2 - 00 55
c.w.
50¢

This book may be kept

FOURTEEN DAYS

A fine will be charged for each day the book is kept overtime.

OCT 25 '82			
GAYLORD 142			PRINTED IN U.S.A.

HOW TO BECOME A CHRISTIAN

HOW TO
BECOME A
CHRISTIAN

SAMUEL M. SHOEMAKER, 1893-

HARPER & BROTHERS, PUBLISHERS
New York

To My Friend and Bishop
Austin Pardue
whose life is a much better
treatise than my book on
how to become a Christian

CONTENTS

CONTENTS

FOREWORD

Some time ago Mr. John Chambers of Harper & Brothers asked me to do a book on "How to Become a Christian." The thought has lain in my mind and I have been gathering material for it.

An invitation from the Bishop of Dallas, Dr. Avery Mason, to conduct a mission in Fort Worth and Dallas in October and November, 1952, gave impetus to putting the material together in spoken form. This book is substantially the addresses which were given in the Texas mission.

I think that there are what might be called "organic" and "inorganic" books. Inorganic books may tell the truth, they may be scholarly, they may help to point the way. They are guides to the mind. But organic books are those which help to set in motion or to sustain actual religious experience. Books concerning the "how" of the Christian life are important chiefly in getting people started—launching them into a dynamic Christian life. They speak to the will. They encourage and try to set in motion those experiments which result in a living faith.

Recently a young man of brilliant mind told me that for years he had tried to find God by reason alone. But he discovered there were reasons against believing, as well as reasons in favor of it. Then he found out that there was another way of approaching belief in God, and that was to put oneself in the way of finding Him through spiritual experiment. He had tried that experiment, and in rather a surprisingly short time he has become a profound and very persuasive believer. It was the contents of this book, given in a small informal group of younger marrieds in my new parish in Pittsburgh, which helped him set this experiment in motion. It is my hope that what I have written, and what my friends at Harper's are giving permanence in print, may help others to find the new life in God through Christ which he has found.

S. M. S.

HOW TO BECOME A CHRISTIAN

1

WHERE WE ARE TODAY

Let us begin by trying to make an honest assessment of where we find ourselves today.

Beginning with the larger picture, the world is now ranged into two vast camps—the camp of those controlled by the Communist power, and the camp of the still free nations. The number of those who pass under the Communist domination is known to be about a hundred million a year—a terrifying figure. The program of Communism includes making hungry and illiterate people believe that Communism means it when it promises them the moon; nor is it hard for the Communists to trade upon the mistakes and omissions of the rich Western nations in their relation to the poorer nations of the East. Communism does not fulfill these promises, of course, but that is discovered only later, too late, and after freedom has gone. Four-fifths of mankind are dark or yellow-skinned; most of them are poor. These people represent Communism's supreme opportunity to bid for the loyalty of the larger portion of humanity. (Herbert Agar reminded us years ago, in *Time for Greatness*, that the white race is the real human minority, being but one-fifth of the total.) And so, as Dr. Karlis Leyasmeyer has pointed out, twenty-five million Communists are taking the world, and six hundred million Christians are letting it go. Says Dr. Frank Laubach, one of the few men today with a world plan and program adequate for these times, "I believe that if the Communists succeed in winning and enslaving two-thirds of the human race as they are doing in the satellite countries now, we shall be enslaved and you and I shall be shot. They can be whipped into mad hate and they can be taught to shoot."

In this world situation, America finds itself with the leadership of the free world on its doorstep. We did not want it, thirty years ago we tried to sidestep it, but destiny has put it there. We are not much trained or experienced in these matters, having been relatively self-sufficient and self-sustained in the past. This may explain our remarkable capacity to win a war and then lose the ensuing peace. The time calls for extraordinary leadership, for a kind of greatness that needs to extend to every citizen. The responsibility today falls, not only on statesmen, but on every person at home who through his vote and influence affects the nation, and on every person who sets foot on foreign soil, for he is an ambassador of freedom and of the Christian world which stands behind freedom. Unless America is a nation that is strong in moral and spiritual stature, relying on the God on whom our fathers relied, we cannot hope to measure up to that which destiny seems to expect of us. We need military and industrial and diplomatic strength, but none of these, nor all of them taken together, is all that we need today.

Sometimes it almost seems to me that the life has gone out of the soul of America. Freedom, once our cause and our passion, is today our right and our indulgence. Something must happen to the inner soul of this nation that is as revolutionary as what has happened to the Communist-dominated countries. Theirs was an imposed revolution, thrust upon them from without. We need a voluntary revolution, imposed upon us by ourselves. We must see clearly where the evils of the world lie, and know the monstrous and demonic evil of Communism for what it is and for what it means to do to enslave mankind. But we must also see clearly where the evils of America lie, and recognize the corruption and compromise and materialism and godlessness that have eaten into the spirit of our nation. These things from within, quite as much as Communism from without, can and, unless checked, will destroy us. They *are* destroying us. They blind our eyes to the truth. They put rope where our spines ought to be. They drag down our youth. They break apart our homes. They create the very demoralized condition which Communism wants as a prelude to their advance upon us. Their strategy is to trade upon poverty where people are poor, and to corrupt and demoralize them when they have enough. Unless America sees this demoralization as of equal seriousness with the threat of Communism, we may be through. Our first line of defense in a free republic is the character and faith of our people. Without these, we are defenseless against the black and evil religion of Communism.

Turning now to the more personal world in ourselves, what do we find? Often we find either a vacuum with no strong belief and no real convictions, or else hopelessly inadequate answers to the problems we face, notably in the area of human nature and human relationships.

The inner life of many people is simply vacant. They may once have had a faith to give life coherence and meaning. But the widespread materialism about them, and the corrosions of a secularistic philosophy in education, have robbed them of it. The cheap, irresponsible materialists, and the clever but unwise educators seem to have formed a coalition bent on drawing down the minds of the oncoming generations from the beliefs and values on which great living depends, and reducing them to concern for what they can possess and feel and touch and enjoy. Great numbers of people still think that only stupid and illiterate folk "believe" in anything, and that clever, educated people have been emancipated from the confinements and superstition of faith. Many of our emotions and values remain Christian (Chesterton said that we are psychological Christians even when we are not theological ones), but in the end these go by the board, too; for unless something in the universe sustains and sanctions them, such things are mere gossamer, the fiction of man's undependable feelings. So we fill our hands and our time with all kinds of activity to make us forget, while our souls are empty of those convictions and standards which alone give life purpose or direction. People turn to pleasure, business, radio and television, sex, drink, drugs, anything to while away a leisure hour, and forget the yawning vacuum that gapes in the place where their souls ought to be. The body dies at our death, and the soul alone survives. Yet we stuff the body and starve the soul, living for the moment and forgetting eternity.

Dr. Farmer, in his book *Servant of the Word*, gives five elements which mark our present state: (1) futility and meaninglessness—life has no framework, no belief, therefore there is no great adventure or purpose; (2) personal insignificance—if the universe is just a vast, cold machine, and all things are measurable in terms of quantity, what are we, what do we matter, what can we do that is worth doing?; (3) yearning for security—we try all kinds of material security because we are so insecure spiritually, but they are no substitute; (4) awareness of the power of evil and unreason—who would have thought that Hitler and Stalin, two of the most barbaric figures ever to stain the page of history, could have arisen in our neat little liberal world of a few years ago, with the most stupendous plans for the enslavement of peoples, and gotten so far with their plans?; (5) the need for an absolute in conduct—experimentalism in moral matters has certainly brought more disaster than blessing, and we flounder for spiritual truth and moral absolutes.

The world situation looks dark. We know there is something terribly missing in personal life. What do we do in face of these things?

Some people give it up, say life is impossible of solution, and just go pagan in a big way. If the future is dark, let us use the present for all it is worth. *Carpe diem.* There are a lot of immediate pleasures, not all of them unsocial either. One can get real pleasure out of food, money, sex, business, travel, reading or good theater. Let's put behind us the old taboos and get as much out of life as we can. You don't need to occupy your mind too much with thinking. Just live. Trust your instincts, etc. The trouble is, however, as Dr. Elton Trueblood says of such people, "They get what they seek, but it is not so attractive in possession as it is in prospect. They think they are emancipated when they are merely unbuttoned.

They have the spurious freedom of one who does not know where he is going or to what he belongs."

Some look for a solution through education and science. I heard a college president say many years ago, "Education will save the world." I thought it was a lie then. I know it is a lie now. Education in the ordinary sense has nothing with which to subdue and tame the raw instincts of man. It is not enlightenment that we need alone, but transformation. Dr. George Buttrick, in his book *Faith and Education*, says,* "recent education has almost deified an attitude of suspended judgment," but he says you "cannot suspend judgment on whether to steal or be honest, or on whether man is a mechanism or a soul." Dr. Buttrick also says that the real aim of education "cannot be different from the total purpose of life," and that the "major question that education must face . . . is God, for if God is the sovereign fact of life, God is the sovereign fact of education. . . . If God is, education must live under the acknowledgement of God." So that unless we add the word "Christian" to education, we have no adequate solution to our problem. Men do not only need facts: they need the interpretation of facts, which involves faith, for no value emerges from facts alone, nor do facts arrange themselves in any meaningful pattern. Education of the kind we have been see-

* Abingdon-Cokesbury. Quoted in *Time*, May 19, 1952.

ing lately will *not* save the world. Life itself demands much more than our professors have been giving to our youth.

Some turn to subversive philosophies because they do not know where else to turn. Seeing too often a spineless church, unwilling to face or grapple with pressing human and moral issues, they look elsewhere. Whittaker Chambers has made it very clear in *Witness* that the world crisis is what makes Communists out of many modern intellectuals. They see no help elsewhere for such things as racial injustice, recurrent financial depressions, and war. They see the evils which persist under capitalism, and for these they would destroy the system, the freedom which is its best element, as well as the wrongs which are its worst. It is as if a man should tear down his house because he does not like the paper on the upstairs hallway. We must remember, too, that many of our evils do not grow up out of our system, but out of our selves. These things are not eliminated by Communism, which adds to the other evils tyranny on the part of the rulers and slavery for the ruled. It seems to me these people who look to other than Christian motivation for the renovation of society do not begin to realize what an achievement even such a measure of freedom as we know in the Western world today has been, nor what it has cost, nor how easy it is to vote it away bit by bit through giving more and more hostages to security through the ever-encroaching power of the state. It is tragic to see whole nations pushed behind the iron curtain with no possibility of regaining their freedom in any foreseeable time: how stupid and insane it is to see those who enjoy freedom allowing a gradual repudiation of its whole ethos and effect, beginning with loss of faith in God from whom it comes! Dostoevsky said, "The problem of Communism is not an economic problem. It is the problem of atheism."

Some go on merely with their pursuit of what is called "the American Way." They believe in our American virtues—hard work, ingenuity, tolerance, fair play, and (until recently) self-reliance. Above all they believe in freedom, which is a kind of climate in which these things arise and thrive. They may no longer hold strong theological beliefs. They will tell you with tremendous (but unconscious) pride that they believe in the Golden Rule and the Sermon on the Mount, and live by them in their personal and business life. (As if the greatest of the saints did not find it difficult even to approach these aims!) They do not pray. They do not worship. They do not believe in anything above the human. They have a code, sometimes a pretty good one; but essentially their weakness is that they are living on the moral and spiritual legacies of the past. Their children, being one generation further from these roots, are so much less likely to share in the perpetuation of even this code of decency. And so it comes about that these perfectly respectable and reputable citizens, having actually no faith but a humanistic one, no God to offset life's obvious materiality, are closer somehow to the enemies of our tradition than they are to the tradition itself. Their ostensible *ways* are the ways of freedom, but their underlying *beliefs* are the beliefs or unbeliefs of materialism, i.e., really of atheism. This sounds like a hard thing to say, but I believe you will see how true it is if you think it over. As time goes on, it becomes increasingly clear that the war of our time is a war fundamentally of beliefs. We think force more nearly supreme today than ever: but the fact is, it is ideas that are the real forces. The real war is a war to decide whether God, or man, is the central fact in our world. Many of these people are good humanists. I think myself that humanism is a way station. You move from it, either in the direction of Christianity, from which most of its moral and human values are derived, or in the direction of Communism, for the simple reason that God has been left out, and in the ensuing vacuum people crave some kind of belief, even some kind of absolute. Neutrality becomes impossible. For either God is, or He isn't. If He is, faith follows, and freedom follows faith in time. If He is not, materialism follows, and slavery follows materialism in time. You can pick flaws in this oversimplified explanation of our present situation; but for the working principles of the average person, it puts the issues about as they are. It is no time to split hairs. There are too many in the world who prefer to split heads instead. Where do your own inner beliefs or unbeliefs lie? Are they on the side of Christianity, or tending that way—or are they really closer to the underlying world-view of Communism?

The most hopeful thing in America today is the growing minority that understands these things, and knows with growing certainty that, if we are to keep our freedom, we must deepen our faith. They want some reasonable, workable approach to faith. Let me suggest some lines of thought.

First, there is always upon us the weight of the mystery of life itself. We found ourselves in this world without asking to come. We wakened and grew up in a world which does not explain itself. The cold stars look down at night, and the sun blesses all things by day. Cancer carries off little children, and we cannot bear to think of the unmentionable cruelties of the concentration camps of Siberia. There are sunsets and symphonies, great human loves and loyalties, magnificent achievements in art and science. Eden was a garden, and there is a little of Eden in your garden and mine. What shall we make of the world's saints; are they fools for being what they were and are? Has the world made its best people its worst dupes? What does it all mean, if it means anything? Man is already halfway on his road to religious faith when he begins thinking like this. Neither science nor philosophy offers him any final answers.

Gordon W. Allport points out * that once men saw science trying to make its way in a world held in the grip of theological domination. Now that situation has changed. The modern student finds himself in a world that is held in the grip of scientific domination. He is first exposed to science, organic evolution, man as a biological member of the animal species. He begins to ask: Is this all there is to reality? Is science a full account of things? What about man's imagination and purpose? What about ideals and values? And what about a First Cause behind all this? It seems increasingly clear that science only describes processes, but says nothing of origins or destinies, or of the value of one fact as against another. No man ever fell in love, or wrote a good poem, or threw himself into a lake to save a child, or exiled himself in the heart of Africa like Schweitzer to atone for the white man's sins against the black, without bringing into play forces which science can neither create nor altogether explain. Part of us is like the animals, but not all of us. The more

* *The Individual and His Religion.* Macmillan.

24

we emphasize our animal qualities, the more do we sink to something less than animal, to something more like a *thing*. The more we emphasize the other side of us, the more do we get above the animal and become in a real sense a person. We are finding that exclusive preoccupation with the physical and material aspects of life does not help us arrive at a satisfactory solution of life.

Again, personal need enters into our search for faith. All of us come up against situations we cannot handle in our own strength. Young, happy, well-adjusted, successful people scarcely believe this; but life and the years will bring them to it. A loved one falls desperately ill. Stark failure confronts us in business. Someone's disloyalty disillusions us till we are almost sick from it. We have a pain in our bodies, or a pain in our minds, that we know will not go away easily; we long for some assuagement or solace. We may pray sometimes, and find some relief. But then we often say, "Is it fair to come back to God when I am in a jam, when I have ignored Him while things went well?" There is a ready answer to this. Suppose you had a son who went out to the ends of the earth somewhere, and lost himself, and one day you had a cable from him asking for help—what would you do? Maybe he *has* gone to hell, and been a rotten son—he is still your boy. Chances are you would send him something to get home with, and give him another chance. Don't you think God is at least as good as you are? Much better to come to Him when things are going well, but if it takes a rough spot for you to learn how much you need God, thank Him for the rough spot and come back to Him as quickly as you can! Life is never easy for very long, and our personal needs bring us back to God. The wonder is that He is always there to meet us.

For mature people, who look about them in this day, the world situation and crisis seem to me the greatest spur of all toward faith. We ought to know that freedom is not just a natural condition—by far the majority of men in all history have been actual or virtual slaves. Freedom is a tiny patch of sunlight breaking through the heavy clouds of age-long tyranny. Freedom's blessings have done more to relieve the lot of men than anything else ever has, except the faith from which our freedom sprang. We have not got perfection in our Western world—far from it—but our freedom gives us the possibility of reforming our lives and our society without limit. The best of the West is less than the least of the Kingdom of God, but it is the best man has achieved in government. God is the renewing element in our free world. We must recognize the truth of Felix Morley's words, "The blessings of liberty, which political government may safeguard or destroy but can never itself provide, are therefore intimately connected with personal belief in, and practice of, Christian doctrine. As Paul told the Corinthians also: 'Where the spirit of the Lord is, there is liberty.' " *

The real answer which we seek seems, then, to lie in a rediscovery of living, Christian faith. Whether we consider Communism abroad or paganism in America, we need the Christian faith to overcome the special problems that confront us today, and to meet the ageless human problems that go along with life itself. What shall we make out of life, and how shall we live it? How can we make a decent and free world? No theoretical, classroom answers will suffice. Neither will new and man-made ones, like Communism or the dogmatic secularism so long rife on our campuses, nor the "business-as-usual" thinking of many businessmen. Man must come back to the God who made him, and whom he has disobeyed and forsaken. He must acknowledge that about ninety-nine hundredths of what makes his life valuable, and even tolerable, he owes to the Christian faith. We must renounce our doubts for faith. We must turn our wondering and wistfulness into belief. We must turn ourselves back to God in simple penitence and prayer, knowing that both our eternal salvation and the safety and welfare of this present world depend upon our once more finding God, and making Him the Center of life.

* *The Power in the People.* Van Nostrand. P. 25.

27

Three years ago some of us met a man in his early thirties who was in business in New York. Some friends of his and ours had invited in a company of younger marrieds, and I was talking with them about the relation of our freedom to our faith. This man had grown up in a family where religions was nonexistent, and graduated from one of our great universities. Two or three days after this, he came down with polio. We went to see him in hospital, and let him know that we were praying for him. He was too sick for us to say much to him: we had to carry the situation with him and his wife and small children, as best we could. In a rather inarticulate way, he reached out for faith. His personal need was added to the need he saw about him in the world, and he knew that he was inadequate. He came through surprisingly well, and with considerable rapidity. Soon after Christmas, he appeared at the parish house one day and asked for me. He said, "I don't know what I'm looking for, but I think I'm looking for somebody to thank." I said, "I think I know who you mean. Let's thank Him now." He said, "I'm not very good at this sort of thing." I told him that didn't matter—what mattered was saying to God what we really felt. I prayed for and with him, then he prayed himself, a simple, real expression of his thanks to God for the beginnings of his recovery. His wife had real faith, and was watching all this process with the greatest interest and with prayer.

He soon came to feel with intensity, young as he was spiritually, that Jesus is the center and heart of Christianity. He couldn't learn enough about Him, couldn't hear His Name often enough, couldn't hear enough witness to what He had done for others. He was baptized and confirmed. One day he came to see me again, saying, "Do you think it's too late for me to get into some kind of service? Business doesn't look very important to me after all that's happened." I asked him whether he was sure it was social service he wanted, or was it the ministry. "I thought it was too late for that," he said; for he had a wife and two children, no savings and no private income. I said of course it was not too late. He talked with the bishop, and the decision was soon made. Two years ago I met him on the train one day coming from a seminary where he'd just been accepted. In a crowded community, God had led him to a house where they could live, instead of his family going off to live with his wife's people. He had, at the eleventh hour, picked up a job in the near-by university co-operative, when jobs were very scarce. The means for his study have been provided. He has lived ever since in an atmosphere where faith is the climate, and personal miracles of God's provision and guidance are the fruit. What a difference from three years ago! A nice, industrious, materialistic pagan, living off the good things God has given this well-blessed nation—and today nearly ready to take up leadership in the Church, in order that he may repay something of what God has done for him and for his country.

Not all will be led into the ministry. But America needs tens of millions of men and women who will take with him the trek from paganism to faith, from aimlessness to purpose, from self-centered to God-centered living. It starts with individual decision to follow Christ. Pagans are the cause of our distraught world. Believing and practicing Christians are the cure for it.

2

THE PROBLEM, THE PERSON, AND THE POWER

If I were to draw a diagram of the structure of what I want to say now, it would be in the form of a Y. I want to deal with three subjects which are really three aspects of one subject. The first two may seem separate at first: they come together as the two top strokes come together to form the one at the base.

First, the *problem*.

Our most immediate problem seems to be life as we find it today. We are in difficulty in two great areas—the world about us, the world of politics and social and international relations; and the world within us, the world of values and beliefs and emotions. Probably the world has always been more or less in turmoil. History knows very few periods in which there has been anything like peace for very long. For peace itself breeds its own kind of lethargy and unwatchfulness, in which more problems gather. But our time seems especially vexing, because of two things: (1) the optimism which false education and false science raised in our minds earlier in this century, as

31

to man's possibilities of creating a fair and decent world by his own wisdom, and which has been so rudely shattered in recent years; and (2) the increasing interconnectedness of the world, which makes danger today like fire in a village of wooden shanties, where one outbreak can cause the destruction of the lot. We have seen the best-educated men in the most privileged nations consistently outwitted by men of barbaric intentions who have put the rest of the world on the defensive. If we are honest, we know that not all the trouble stems from godless and materialistic Communists; it stems also from godless and materialistic men everywhere, and we have got vast hordes of them right here in our own country. That we seem able to do so little to better our world, when our knowledge and technical skills are so great, is a baffling and frustrating experience.

Inwardly we live in constant awareness of what destruction might be wrought in the earth if all the physical energy man has at his disposal were released. We do not know whether this atomic age is going to be one in which there is greater prosperity and leisure, or whether we shall all be blown up. The effect of living in times like these is hard on our emotions. Add to this the fact that many of our educational institutions have exposed our young people to nothing but a secularistic, naturalistic view of life, and robbed them of the powerful spiritual resources which alone come to the rescue of our emotional difficulties, and you need not wonder at narcotics and crime and despair in so many of the youth of our time.

But the real problem is not "life as we find it today"; it is life itself. Life and the world have always been problems. We find ourselves alive on this physical earth. Is it a tragedy, or an opportunity, or does it mean just nothing? Is the world an oyster in which to dig pearls, or a school where we are meant to learn something? Is the physical really all there is, as the Communists believe; or is the spirit real? Are people like Kagawa and Schweitzer and Laubach saints, or are they saps? Or are the Americans, who see nothing beyond material success, the saps? There is nothing lying round on the face of life, like a map at a gas station, to tell you what life is or how to live it. From within it arise men of reason, wisdom, inspiration. From within it arise also gangsters, idiots, Communists. Life itself is the problem, always has been the problem, always will be the problem. I once heard the great English scholar, the late Dr. B. H. Streeter of Oxford, say that he never got anywhere while he just considered Christianity the problem, and tried to answer the questions it raises; when he began seeing that life was the problem, life asked the questions, and Christianity was the effort to answer the questions and meet the problem, then he began getting somewhere. Life is the problem. What does life itself mean, and how are we meant to live it?

Second, the *Person*.

More than nineteen hundred years ago there appeared on this earth a man. He was a human being like all the others, with a body and a life. There was nothing eerie or peculiar about Him. He came into a human home and was brought up there and got the education His people got. He was probably a carpenter by trade. He worked as a laborer in the town where His family lived till He was about thirty. Then He started out on an itinerant movement, preaching to people wherever they would listen, and healing many by laying His hands on them and praying for them. Building on what He received from His own inherited religion, He went far beyond it. The manifestation of spiritual power and the open challenge to the pious as well as the pagans of His day brought Him in conflict with the religious leaders. The political forces feared Him because of His potential threat to Rome. So they got together and crucified Him. But the company of people who believed in Him were sure that He came back from the dead, and they saw Him too often to doubt the fact that He had risen from the grave.

What to make of Him? Even when He was here, people

noticed something extraordinary about Him. They did not miss anything that healthy, human men possess, but they found something that went far beyond what other men possess. It set them wondering who this was. He did not discourage this inquiry; at times He fomented it. As one sees the development of this question through the four Gospels, it becomes clear that He was seeking to get His companions to recognize this unique thing about Him, without quite telling them what it was. At Caesarea Philippi He asked them who men were saying that He was, and then He asked them who they thought He was. And Simon Peter, presumably speaking for them all, said, "Thou art the Christ, the Son of the living God." If that had been said about you or me, because people saw spiritual power in us, we should have said, "Peter, don't talk blasphemy." That is not what Jesus said. He said, "Blessed art thou, Simon son of Jonah, for flesh and blood hath not revealed it unto thee, but my Father which is in heaven." And then He proceeded to say that He would found His Church upon the faith that Simon articulated.

Moreover, His death was something more than a good man dying for a cause. He did not say very much of the deeper meaning of His death, but He said enough to set us wondering. He used words like "ransom" and "remission of sins" in connection with it. Later St. Paul's great mind went to work on the Cross, and the fully developed doctrine of the Atonement was the result. It became the astonishing faith of Christians that what men had dimly sought after through all the ages, through the sacrifice of animals and even other human beings, something to expiate and make up for those sins of ours which nothing seems to cleanse—this had been fulfilled and satisfied in the death of Jesus. He had died for the sins of man. He had offered to God such a perfect sacrifice of Himself that God's holiness was satisfied and God's love was manifested to all men; and our redemption was complete. It is hard to understand the Cross altogether in its deeper aspects, for it has to do with the whole relation of the holy and loving God to us in our sins, and what Christ did to open the way again for man in his relation to God. But "we believe it was for us, He hung and suffered there."

With every further step in His life, we are carried into a deeper mystery. Greatest and most important of all is the mystery of the Resurrection. He had promised that it would happen. The gloom of Good Friday was so great that it seemed to blot out even the memory of Christ's own promise that He would rise again. When the word came that some of the women, then some of the apostles, had seen Him, they were incredulous. But there was gathering evidence of two kinds: (1) that His disciples saw Him, on one occasion more than five hundred of them together; and (2) that if there had been no resurrection, how does one account for the reunion of the apostles and the continuing of the Church; or for the Holy Communion, which is not the memorial of a dead Lord but the feast of a living one; or for the changing of the Sabbath to Sunday, as the day in the week when men rest and worship, remembering that Sunday is the day of the Resurrection? The Resurrection became the cardinal and paramount article of faith for the early Church and for the Church ever since.

He was finally withdrawn from their sight by the Ascension. The days of His flesh were finished. He was back again in the glory from which He came.

If Jesus were just an ordinary man, a spiritual reformer with a pure spirit and intention, it would be folly to talk about Him as being hung on a Cross for the sins of the world, or to call Him the Son of God in the unique sense in which that phrase is used of Him, or to think that He had overcome death and risen from the dead. But if it should be that He was what He more than hinted, and what His early followers believed Him to be, then that puts another face on everything. It is the combined testimony of the earliest writings of the New Testament, of the historic Church throughout the ages, and of all those countless millions of people who have accepted Him on His own terms, and found life enhanced beyond description as a result, that He is the Divine Saviour of the world, unique, of one substance with the Father, "God of God, Light of Light, very God of very God, begotten not made," as the Nicene Creed says of Him.

The late Archbishop Temple, one of the outstanding scholars as well as statesmen of our day, said (in his *Readings in St. John's Gospel*), "It is now recognized that the only Christ for whose existence there is any evidence at all is a miraculous Figure making stupendous claims." *

Concerning the divinity of Jesus, C. S. Lewis puts the issues in simple, epigrammatic form. "I am trying," he says, "to prevent anyone from saying the really silly thing that people often say about Him: 'I'm ready to accept Jesus as a great moral teacher, but I don't accept His claim to be God.' That's the one thing we mustn't say. A man who was merely a man and said the sort of things Jesus said wouldn't be a great moral teacher. He'd be either a lunatic—on a level with a man who says he's a poached egg—or else he'd be the Devil of hell. You must make your choice. Either this man was, and is, the Son of God, or else a madman or something worse. You can shut Him up for a fool, you can spit at Him and kill Him for a demon; or you can fall at His feet and call Him Lord and God. But don't let us come with any patronizing

* Macmillan. P. xxiv.

nonsense about His being a great human teacher. He hasn't left that open to us."

Third, the *power*.

When the Person comes in contact with the problem, there power is born, as when steel strikes stone a spark results. When man recognizes the situation of his estrangement from God, and the trouble that has come into the world since "man's first disobedience and the fall," then the process of redemption begins working within the process of creation. Christ comes right into the midst of man's predicament, and sets about helping him. The Creator-God goes into action as the Redeemer-God.

Oftentimes we are little conscious of the problem of life in its larger cosmic setting, and only dimly conscious of the Person of Christ, until we see His power touch life at some visible, and urgent, point.

Look backward and see what happens when this Person goes to work on the pagan outlook. Because there is no God in it, the pagan outlook reduces man to his own powers. Pagans, as we find them in America today and in a society where there are marks and influences of Christianity, are more decent and a great deal happier than they were in Greece or in Rome. Much of what they enjoy has been created by others with a different outlook. Simple, long-standing, natural paganism is gray with depression. It must talk about "fate" because it cannot talk about "God." It has gods, but it knows they are fictions. Modern paganism comes to worship idols of its own making—money and sex and power. The gods of paganism in Christ's day were as dead as the clay figures I used to see rotting away in Chinese temples. Then Christ comes! And with Him comes faith in one pure and loving God. With Him comes faith in a purpose in life—not a cyclic, monotonous round of senseless events, but an emerging plan. With Him comes a sense of personal, human worth, based on our sonship to God Himself. With Him comes a joy in the adventure of living that can only exist where we feel in personal relation to God. And official paganism was outmoded and left behind.

Yet paganism is recurrent. Paganism is the next step after secularism. Once you are without God, you slide down into paganism inevitably. There are some fine way stations on the path, and you will meet excellent people in them. But their children will be the full-blown product—unless the children have the wit to see that their parents lacked something, and that whatever else the parents gave them, they did not give them the greatest essential of all. Someone said that an atheist is a man with no invisible means of support. We all need invisible means of support, and without them we are poor. America is full of people, living on the blessings and benefits of

Christian civilization, who never stop to think that this all came from something—we should not have freedom and human rights as we do, had not a faith once given them birth. How shall these things continue without the faith that nurtures them? Let people get soggy with the comfort that Western civilization makes possible for them, and they will slowly vote away to government the very freedom that they indulge, unless there is a return of faith that will again put foundations under our freedom.

What happens when the Person touches the problem of human wrong and injustice? Take the matter of slavery, for instance, which was accepted as inevitable by the Greeks and Romans. Christ puts man in a certain relation to God. That begins at once to affect his relation with his fellows. Christ puts values in man's heart, human values, Christian values. I have an old Bible in German, printed in Zurich in 1538. It belonged to one of my ancestors, Gerhard Hendricks, who came out with William Penn in 1685. In 1688, Gerhard Hendricks signed as the first name on the first petition against slavery ever written in this country: that petition is in the old Arch Street Meetinghouse of the Friends, in Philadelphia. I venerate that old book with its finger-stained edges and pages, not only from family sentiment, but because that man found he could not read those words and countenance men's ownership of other men.

What happens when the Person touches the problem of government? The easiest solution is to let the strong take the helm in human society and hold it as long as they can. That does not satisfy the Christian conscience. If men are what Christ taught they were, then government must reflect and manifest the Christian values. Christianity dares to envision a situation where we choose our own rulers, and where they are accountable to the people. Democracy, as William Allen White once said, is a rough attempt to institutionalize the Christian religion. Democracy does not work perfectly—Western civilization is not Utopia—but we are safe in saying that the more Christianity there is in society, the better democracy works. We owe the whole experiment in freedom and democracy to the Christian tradition. All our blessings in the realm of freedom are attributable to Christ. The power of Christ, in His effect on history, is about us at every turn of our daily life.

But these larger problems of social injustices and the need for political reform are often touched by the medium of remade persons. It is when the Person touches the immediate, personal problems of your life and mine that His power is made most evident.

Look, for instance, at the astonishing movement called

Alcoholics Anonymous. It happened that the founding spirit of that group found God and a new way of life in Calvary Church, New York, nearly twenty years ago. He was himself an alcoholic, helpless in the grip of his addiction. Then the miracle happened. The Person met the problem, and power was born. He became a new man, and his home a new home. Seeing two other men who had been helped, he realized that here was not an accident but law. He went to work to discover what it was, talking with doctors, psychiatrists, parsons, and re-covered alcoholics themselves. He seemed to "see" with a flash of prophetic insight what could happen if this began to spread by the contagion of the lives and witness of recovered men and women. Today they number in the hundreds of thousands, new men, new women, new businesses, new homes. And all because they have learned that there is in the world a Higher Power on whom they can call in their desperation.

Many people who are not alcoholics seem to think that this profound transformation is very necessary for drunks, but not at all necessary for ordinary decent folk. I think A. A. has a great deal to say to us all. There are thousands in this world who do not get drunk on alcohol, but they get very drunk on fear and self-pity and depres-sion and a desire to have their own way in life. A man who returns home in a cantankerous mood in the evening, a woman determined to use her ailments as a way of getting attention and service, are both drunk—one on moods, the other on self-centeredness.

A woman came in great inward need. Her home was broken, and her life was broken. She met some changed people, some people trying to be Christians. She stayed close enough to them to begin to catch fire from them, as a stick will do when you keep it close to the flame. She tried to face what had been wrong in herself, as well as in her husband. She committed her life to Christ in faith. She began turning a conventional, inherited faith into a living faith. She began praying and learning how to wait on God till His power comes through. Then the time came for her to go home. She went back to her church, but she needed something more personal than that sometimes provides. She was given the name of another woman in her locality whose life had also been profoundly transformed by Christ. Then she wrote, "She and I got together Thursday night and again last night for prayer. We plan to meet twice a week. . . . I had my first call for help yesterday, someone who has had the same experience I have had. When called, I prayed over it and then went over. I took her two little booklets and tried to pass on to her what God had given me. I was so conscious all the time of what Dr. Whiston said, 'God brings definite people to us for help.' We got along beautifully and I could honestly tell her that God does give us peace of mind and soul if we trust Him. I know that He gives us this help, not to keep but to share with others. I am hopeful she will join the other two of us for prayer. I promised, when I was at Calvary, that I would never say 'no' when someone called for help, and I promise again, I will always go, after taking it to God first. Then I know He will give the help they want through me. . . . I have my bad times but they are farther and farther apart and I know I am all right now. I have *found* the Way. I know you are praying for me, I feel it, and know you will continue. I need your prayers, but I know that everything is going to be all right." She could have turned into a self-centered, self-pitying divorcee, without God, without hope, but instead she has turned into a Christian with faith and purpose and able to be used in the lives of others in need as she was. Through persons like that, God pours down His power into the world anew.

A middle-aged couple were living across the square in New York. They were charming pagans. For her beautiful furniture and for him the cocktail shaker were life's priorities. Someone told them there was something going on spiritually over on the corner and they ought to go and see what it was. They came. They met other people whom they liked, and for whom religion was not a tradition but a passion. He looked up a man with whom he could talk out his problems, and she a woman with the same purpose. They made the first steps toward God— facing honestly their own lives, being honest about their sins, committing themselves so far as they could to as much of Christ as they understood. Prayer became real to them. They began studying the Bible. They were con- firmed and joined the church. They began reaching out to their friends and acquaintances with a dynamic faith. The adventure of it all was evident to any who saw them. Their close friends became Christians, not pagans, but they kept in touch with pagans, kept on loving them, and began reaching them for Christ. They have lost com- pletely all shyness about speaking of these things. Shy- ness usually means you are pretty shy on religion itself. When your heart gets full of it, so too does your talk. You don't talk dogmatically or self-righteously, but you lard your spiritual experience into your ordinary talk, and people get intrigued. Down in the countryside where they now live, this couple are known and loved for being the cheerful Christians they are. You may find him looking after his sheep or his pigs, or you may hear him lead a service in the old church as a lay reader when the parson is away, or you may see him talking with some- body about the needs of his life while leaning on his hoe. There are the world's great saints, and then there are the people like this whose lives, apart from Christ, are just as hard to explain as St. Paul's or St. Francis'. You do not need to be long with them to feel the power.

But it is not *their* power. It is when the Person—the Person of all time, of all history, of the very universe itself, the Person Christ—touches the problem of life—of life as a whole, of your life and my life with their immediate problems—that the spark of spiritual power is struck. For that power the world starves. Without that power we go astray, we miss the meaning of life, we flounder and make mistakes and get into difficulty and draw others into the same difficulty with us. That Christ is waiting to change your life if you will let Him.

3

HUMAN NEED

Mankind, for the past half-century, has been behaving like a bumptious adolescent schoolboy, swaggering with new-felt power, tackling somebody too big for him and coming off with a bloody nose and some broken bones. We have been confidently telling ourselves that we were perfectly able to manage our affairs, and we have been showing by the results that we were not. Education on the whole, secularistic and naturalistic views of life, and man's native and irrepressible pride have all combined to assure us of our competence. And we have brought the world closer to absolute ruin than any generation has ever been.

There isn't any doubt about our new-found powers. We can send messages faster, we can travel more quickly, we can produce more goods and gadgets, we have made life more healthy and more comfortable than any age has ever been able to do. The climax has been the release of atomic energy. It is as if the final stage in the career of the adolescent was not his control by some new power within himself, but the putting in his hands of a force great enough to destroy himself and everybody round him. It is a bromide by now that our scientific progress has far outrun our moral and social progress. Yet all these new-found powers could be used to make life better if only we ourselves were better. For instance, grinding toil that used to break men up and turn young men into old ones has been replaced in countless places by machinery which lessens the muscular labor men must exert. We ought to be better men for it. We must become better men if we are to use these things in a constructive, not in a destructive, way.

But that is just the trouble. If you know the combination, you can exercise control over nature. What is the combination that can control man? The Nazis and the Communists had their combination: they would turn him into a slave, tell him what to do and think, and, if he did not obey, punish and torture him or his family with indescribable cruelties. We may be sure that no society will let unbridled lawlessness go on forever. Some strong hand will reach up and take the reins. He will say that it is to restore law and order, and he will say that he represents the people when he does it; but the raw lust for power that lies deep in the hearts of all men till God changes them profoundly will find the chaos of society a perfect excuse and field for going into action. The world has never seen such dictators as our age has seen. The way they work is to compel men to obey them. The fiction of order which they create only masks the reeking results of their mad drive for power—especially cruel power over other people. That is one way to solve the question of controlling man.

What is the alternative? Is there an alternative—or are we cooped up to the two possibilities, chaos or slavery? This all sounds theoretical to us in free America. It does not sound theoretical in Czechoslovakia or Poland or North China. If the Communist encirclement continues till southern Asia with all its vast populations is in the hands of the Soviets, it will not sound theoretical here. Taking the long look, America and the West—indeed, the whole world—must discover something that can change and control human nature. Man in relation to society must discover something that will give him what Lord Moulton once called "obedience to the unenforceable." Because, of course, true morality is essentially "unenforceable"; it grows up voluntarily out of what we consider to be life's values and therefore its necessary standards.

For this reason, how we *behave* is dependent on what we *believe*. Many people entertain a naïve notion that moral values and standards of practice are something that decent people come by as naturally as they come by eyesight or a sense of smell. So blindly unconscious are most

of us concerning our Christian heritage! For in the somewhat tangled web of Western civilization there are
caught a thousand decencies and values which came originally from Christianity. Toynbee calls ours "Christian
civilization," surely not because we are fully Christian or
ever have been, but because we owe the best we have to
Christianity. You simply cannot pull out the Christian
underpinnings from human morals and expect them to
remain intact. What we believe, really believe, conditions
completely how we behave. Take Germany during the
Nazi terror. If idealism had been enough, the professors
in universities, and the newspaper editors, would have
had the courage to stand up against the fury of the Nazis:
but they all crumpled in the end. The only thing that
stood squarely across Hitler's path and refused to
knuckle was the Christian Church. Einstein said he never
had much use for the Church before that, but that moved
him.

It is important what we believe about ourselves what
we believe about God, and therefore what we believe
about life.

How should we think of ourselves? How does Christianity tell us to think of ourselves? It does not tell us to
think one thing, but to think two things, and to hold
them always in equilibrium. It tells us we are God's children, made in His image, with some of Him in us, as a

51

likeness in a child to a father. It tells us we are all potentially Christian believers and saints. It tells us that we matter to God and are of infinite worth. It also tells us we are often God's disobedient children, often very far from God's image in us. Because we were made free, we were free to obey or to disobey. All of us at some time have chosen the way of disobedience. When we disobey or sin we feel a division run down through us, as if part of us belonged to God, and part to Evil. When man thinks of himself as being satisfactory, all right, and in no need of change, he lets loose the prideful elements in him which can destroy him. When man thinks of himself as beyond hope, needing change but fundamentally incorrigible, he drowns himself in despair. The truth does not lie somewhere in the middle between optimism and pessimism: we ought always to be optimistic insofar as we are God's conscious children, asking for forgiveness again and again; and we ought always to be pessimistic insofar as we are never wholly free from recurrent evil and sin within us. What we need is something to encourage the best in us, while it keeps us humble about the worst in us. As touching my faith in God and my redemption through Christ, the sky is the limit to which I can ascend. As touching my pride in myself and my self-ruled life, hell is the limit to which I can descend. Christianity is the only fully realistic religion in the world, when it comes to the interpretation of human nature.

What do we believe about God? We believe that He is "the Father Almighty, Maker of heaven and earth," all-wise, all-good, and ever-present. We believe He has a will for mankind and the world, and therefore a will for each one of us which it is up to us to try to find. We believe that in some way hard to describe He is *in* history, working out His purposes through the co-operating and even the contrary wills of men. Supremely we believe that God manifested Himself fully in Jesus. "God so loved the world that He gave His only-begotten Son. . . ." Whether we know it or not, the way we think about God, and what we believe concerning Him, we think and believe almost wholly because of Jesus. God gives us freedom, lets us make our own decisions, yet helps us to decide the right way if we ask guidance of Him. We do that with our own children: we let them grow up with a mixture of solicitude for them and letting them alone—otherwise they would never grow up. God has a purpose when He lets us be born. This world is a kind of school where we are being trained. We learn by study, by participation, sometimes by hard knocks. Trouble, tribulation, pain, even sickness and suffering, have been allowed by God. They can't be unmitigatedly evil or He would not have allowed them. Many times we grow by these things. As the Greeks said, we learn by suffering. If that is the price of our growing up and achieving character, God lets it be so. He always deals with us with love as His motive. Sometimes He deals with us by gentleness, and sometimes He deals with us by judgment. God is a Father, responsible, really loving, not a spoiling old grandfather with nothing but candy and a good time. God runs the universe. He wants this world to be what it should. It will not be such till man co-operates with Him. That must be voluntary co-operation, or it means nothing. We find our lives by co-operating with God.

What do we believe about life? If we believe in God, we must believe that life is not a fate but a privilege. One of the grandest things in the Episcopal Prayer Book is the line, "We bless thee for our creation. . . ." We are not put here to have things easy, but to have them right. The object of life is not to be painless, but to be great. That is why so much of our pursuit of comfort is really a pursuit of dope: we hide from reality by comfort, as a man hides from life with heroin or marijuana. If we were put here to be comfortable, then life is a bad job. But if we were put here to be trained, it looks as if life were doing a pretty good job of it. If a man playing football judges the fineness of the game by whether he avoids barking his shins, he will have a bad time of it and play rotten football. You will think life is a bad game unless you find out what its object is, and then play with all your might, regardless of what happens to you in the

54

process. Life calls for thought and philosophy. But still more life calls for purpose and for heroism. If a vast war between Good and Evil is being fought in this universe, my life and the winning of its battles can be a footnote to that great conflict. But if I see life only as a chance to please myself, then I live constantly in sin. That's what sin is—to miss and ignore the purpose of God, and put my own little purposes in place of His.

We need to understand what sin is. You can't draw a circle round an act and label it "sin" or "not sin." You must consider, first, the whole law of God, as indicating what He wants of us, what He means life to be. And you must consider, second, the whole of His will for your life, and ask whether this attitude or act or practice contributes to, or detracts from, this whole big purpose of God. I believe that every man and woman who calls himself or herself by the name of Christian should be a marked person. There ought to be something distinctive and different about them—not self-conscious and prudish, but honest about themselves and humble and obviously in touch with God. More than that, they ought to be carriers and contagious influences for the Christian life, ever alert to help others to know Him and find faith. Chesterton says of the Franciscan brothers that it was their purpose to see that anyone "who met one of them by chance should have a spiritual adventure." That should be the purpose of every Christian. Now it is in the light of that that we should ask whether we drink or smoke, whether we use foul language and tell shady stories, whether we spend ten times on our clothes what we give to the church, whether we are living for the wrong ends and purposes. If you and I are meant to be channels for Christ, the greatest of all sins must be that we should be ineffective for Him—that we find ourselves with people who need faith more than they need bread or medicine or human affection, and yet be unable to get it across to them. Sin is the thing in us that keeps us from being channels of God's power. We can sin just as much through moodiness, or inflexibility of plans, or temper, or resentments, or self-pity, as through adultery or drunkenness. Whatever keeps us from a living, loving relation with other people—or from a vital and open relation with God—is sin. Look at your gambling and your petulance and your love of power, and ask yourself whether they are keeping you from being a force for God. Turn the sins over to God, and let Him take the steam you used to put into them and put it into something useful and constructive that helps build His kingdom.

It would be a very good thing if you took a piece of foolscap paper and wrote down the sins you feel guilty of. Don't make them up—there will be plenty without that. Just the ones you really feel: the temper at home, the sloppiness in caring for your things, the big resentment you must give up, the apology you know you should make but never have. One of the simplest and best rules for self-examination that I know is to use the Four Standards, which Dr. Robert E. Speer said represented the summary of the Sermon on the Mount— Absolute Honesty, Absolute Purity, Absolute Unselfishness, and Absolute Love. Review your life in their light. Put down everything that doesn't measure up. Be ruthlessly, realistically honest. When sin clogs a human soul, it is worse than food clogging a human body, or mud or refuse in a drainpipe. You will be amazed at what a lift it gives you just to face up to these things honestly. Go as far as you can with that.

Now you may find that you get stuck somewhere. You are not sure about something, whether it's a sin or not. Or you wonder what to do next. You may need other human counsel. You may know a mature Christian layman or laywoman to whom you can go and talk these matters out in all frankness and confidence. Pray about who it shall be. Or you may find you need the help of an understanding Christian minister. He is trained to help you, or he ought to be. Tell him what you are thinking and feeling. Dig down where it hurts, and get it all out. Some do this informally, like two people talking in a living room. Some do it formally, through the instrument of Confession. Whichever way you do it, its effectiveness depends on its thoroughness and honesty. If then the minister helps you to pray it out to God in penitence, praying for you and for himself with you, it may be helpful if you ask him, in God's Name, to say the words of Absolution.

There are two important parts of this process. The first is our own honesty in facing and confessing our sins. We very often, indeed I should say usually, need to let some other human being know about us. Why? Aren't we Protestants who believe in no intermediary between us and God? That again is a fine theory, but actually there is nothing which so much gets at the pride which underlies all other sin and pervades it as having to tell the truth about ourselves to another human being. It must be a responsible one who will hold our confidence; it should be done between two people only. But nothing else so demolishes pride as recognizing our need of another person to help us, and the humiliation of having another human being know about us. The A.A.'s say, "Make a fearless moral inventory. Admit to God, to yourself and to another human being the exact nature of your wrongs." That is drastic, but it is effective, principally because it gets at our pride.

The second important part of this is receiving forgiveness. If the Christian religion is true, Jesus Christ went up on the Cross for you and for me. He would have done it if there had been no other sinner in the universe but you or me. "He died that we might be forgiven." The Cross cleared the way back to God. His death atoned for human sin. The apparatus of forgiveness is there. But it is only effective in your life and mine when we accept His forgiveness. You have been honest with yourself, with another human being, and with God. Then what? Then draw up under the Cross of Christ, as a man does under a shelter when it is raining. Look up at Him. You and He are alone there together. It is all a great, objective fact: He died for human sin. It becomes a great, subjective fact when I say to Him, "This hast thou done for me: what have I done for thee?" Stay there with Him till His forgiveness has cleaned you off like a bath after a hot day in the fields. Don't just recall there is such a thing as Christian forgiveness: accept it into your own very soul. Let it take over your mind and your emotions and get down into your subconscious. "I am forgiven through Christ!" Say it to yourself. It covers everything, from murder to malice, if you mean your repentance. Many are haunting psychiatrists' offices for something they will never find there. They can find a better understanding of their own emotional and mental workings; but they cannot find the answer to their feeling of guilt.

Not all guilt is artificial and unreal: much of it is real and justified. Only Christ's forgiveness brings the answer. If we are truly forgiven by Christ, then we ought both to forgive one another and to forgive ourselves. That is sometimes hard. But we must let up on ourselves and realize that between Christ's Cross and our own genuine repentance there is power enough to create forgiveness that makes new lives in us and puts fresh hope in our hearts. Amid all the sensations that we seek and enjoy in a highly sensuous age, there is one we have missed—it is the feeling of cleanness and freedom that comes to those who know they are forgiven.

I knew a remarkable man, who was for many years at work in the old Gas House District of New York, reaching out to the down-and-outs (and some up-and-outs, too) for Christ. He had little education, and his eyesight was so poor he could read little. I suppose I have heard that man witness to his Christian experience a hundred times, and never heard him do it twice the same. Where did he get the originality, the freshness, for this? He got it from a living wonder that he carried in his heart more than a quarter of a century, a wonder that God had taken notice of him when he was in great need, when he was a bounder of the worst type, and given him new life and forgiveness. He lived in the joy and gratitude of that forgiveness all the rest of his days. Would that all

Christians knew the source of his joy and power and lasting enthusiasm!

There is another part of getting right. We must try to get right with other people, as well as with God. Again I quote the A.A.'s: "Make a list of all persons you have harmed, and become willing to make amends to them all. Make direct amends to such people wherever possible, except when to do so would injure them or others." Now and then you find people who, when they begin the Christian life, want to begin as of this date. They want to let bygones be bygones, and not "rake up" old scores. The trouble with this is that it will not work, and it will not work because it is not honest. "Forgive us our trespasses as we forgive those who trespass against us." Do we want to be forgiven as we forgive others? If so, we had better get busy doing some wholesale forgiving all round. None of this "waiting till they come to me" business. We are not in a mood of forgiveness unless we are in a mood of *forgivingness*—and that means being willing to take the first step toward reconciliation. If there is an old, long-standing bitterness in your life against someone, pray about that person, and when your spirit is right go and make amends. Nothing else will release you, maybe nothing else will release him, into freedom and health of mind and body.

So much of our sickness of mind and body is spiritual.

Not all of it—some is organic—but who will say that even this has not been helped on by self-pity, loneliness (which means lack of love for others), resentments, hates, or fears? I heard a wonderful story a while ago about a man in Canada who is greatly used by God, Dr. Albert Cliffe. He was out somewhere in western Canada, and a woman came to him for healing of arthritis. He asked her against whom she was holding resentment. It was her sister. When their father died he had left the bulk of his estate to the sister, and a pittance to her. She resented it, and resented the sister. Dr. Cliffe said he could do nothing for her till her resentment was cleared up, and he would pray for her that she rid herself of it and repair the relation between herself and her sister. In a short time, she went to her sister, shared her grievance, made amends for her resentment. And then what do you think happened? Her arthritis began to disappear, of course—but something else. Her sister went to the lawyer and had him divide the estate exactly in half, so that both had the same amount! We do not always come out advantageously materially, when we are honest with people in that way, but we always come out advantageously as to health and restored human relations. We talk a lot about our crosses: the only really saving cross most of us will ever experience is the cross that runs a minus sign right through the big "I" and cancels it out. I know a man today who is professionally a Christian, but he is a sick, failing, and tragic man. I don't know all of the causes, but I know in part it goes back to his refusal to apologize to a garage man with whom he lost his temper a great many years ago.

One reason why the Christian religion has been so salutary for mankind is that it has known just where to lift man up, and just where to keep him down. When he is discouraged, caught in his sins, "sunk" about himself, Christianity offers him hope and forgiveness. But when he is full of himself and his importance, when his pride runs away and lifts him up about his own virtues and achievements, Christianity reminds him who he is. Christianity always "puts down the mighty from their seat, and exalts the humble and meek." It levels up man's despair about himself, and levels down his pride.

In this day of crisis and urgency, we all look for great solutions and we know we must not delay about them. This tends to put all the stress on big human plans, military, industrial, political. They are all important. But something else is important, also, the inner life of people, what they believe about God and life and themselves. In the end, the outer world is a pretty faithful reproduction of the inner world. We cannot hope to make a world of righteousness and peace while the souls of our people are full of sin and of conflict. Our solution does not lie wholly with the big human plans: it lies also in creating new men and women, in the only way in which they can be created, namely, by the transforming power of Jesus Christ. When a man becomes a Christian he is doing more than finding a solution for his own life—he is contributing to the reservoir of moral and spiritual strength without which material strength means little. We see the importance of our production plants. But all our churches ought to be production plants for the turning out of new men and women, and if we were doing what we should, they would be; and wherever we are even beginning to do this, they are already. In the end it all comes back to the honesty with which we face our sins, give them to God, make them right where we can with those whom we have hurt, accept God's forgiveness, and step out into the clear stream of God's grace and the new life He gives to those who ask it from Him.

4

THE NEW BIRTH

How does a person get started on a genuine Christian experience? We have seen enough of people for whom religion is just tradition, or just ceremony. We have been too long like that ourselves. How can we move out of that into spiritual reality? If we can get the question of "how" answered for people, we shall have them halfway in it already.

The first thing is to come in touch with religion where it is vital, where power is being generated and released. One of the reasons why religion has been a strong factor in Yale University is that for many years there has been a place called the Yale Hope Mission, where needy men get converted. Something happens. In some churches it seems as if nothing ever happens. If it did, somebody would stand up and try to quiet it down. What chance has God got in a place like that? But go to an A.A. meeting, or join my friend Ralston Young, Red Cap 42, in Grand Central Station, New York, when he is having one of his noon meetings in an empty car on Track 13, Monday, Wednesdays, and Fridays, and you will see religion at work, religion as power and joy and adventure.

The second thing is to acknowledge your own need. You can't just walk into the fifteenth story of a building: you have to remember you are on ground level and need to climb up. If you think you are pretty good as you are, then you will stay as you are. If you are dissatisfied with yourself—not with other people, nor with life and the world, but with yourself—you run a chance of getting somewhere. In proportion to your sense of conscious need you will seek an adequate answer. Christ is adequate all right, but He never can do much for the self-satisfied. If you come by a good old red-hot conviction of sin, it will do you more good than all the little soft religious reading you will ever get out of some of the comfortable counsel that comes in promised booklets offered over the radio. We need a Gospel that speaks to our condition. We are sinners, as men have always been—not fiction sinners, not *pro forma* sinners, but real sinners, away from God, estranged from Him by our own disobedience and rebellion. Ask yourself how much of your deep, inner, invisible private life is taken up with sex, with ego-satisfaction, or the pursuit of sheer physical comfort. When have you helped anyone find Christ? Let a man or woman honestly answer that, and then go on pretending he or she is not in any need of reformation or redemption! The desperation of our world is the reflection of our desperate inner need.

The third thing is to make a definite Christian decision. There are two parts to Christian conversion; there is God's part, and there is our part. You sometimes hear it said that "religion is what a man does with his solitude." But that is not true if he is a Christian: for then religion is not what man does with his solitude, but what God does with man's self-estrangement. He has already made the great move in our direction. He came in Christ. Christ remains His standing invitation to the world. Christ was God's first move toward us in our estrangement from Him. Whenever anybody finds God and becomes a real Christian, most of the work is done from God's side. No man can redeem himself. No man can make a cross of his own that saves him. The Divine Initiative comes first. "By grace ye are saved through faith." That verse says it all. It is grace, not gumption or glands or goodness, that saves us.

But grace saves "through faith." Grace is God's part. Faith is man's part. What is faith? Well, what is faith in a person? You have faith in a doctor, that when he puts you under an anaesthetic and cuts into your body he will do the wise and right thing. You have faith in a lawyer, that you can commit your case to him and he will handle it wisely and well. Faith is a belief in someone's integrity and capacity. You can trust him. Faith in God is like that. It has intellectual factors in it, but it also has in it a preponderance of loyalty, of confidence, of active trust. Sometimes we think faith is given to some people and not to others, like an ear for music, or a striking personality. Faith is much more like falling in love, which can come to anybody. Faith does not so much depend on my capacity to give it as on the other person's capacity to arouse it. It is like admiration: I can't just will to admire someone, but if he or she is admirable, neither can I withhold my admiration. It is just so with faith. It is my belief that nobody can stay around our Lord Jesus Christ very long without coming to believe in Him. The faith is mine, but it is provoked by Him. Faith is my response to Him.

We must make a distinction between "faith" and "the faith." "The faith" is the whole of that body of revealed truth that has come to us in the Christian revelation. Don't try to start with this—if you do, you will get spiritual indigestion. Start with faith in Christ; and through Christ your mind will be led and widened out into the vast, rich truths that He taught and the Church has taught in His Name. Don't try at first to understand all the intricacies of the doctrine of the Holy Trinity, or some of the other things in the Creed that trouble you. Begin with faith in Christ Himself. Once you get clear on Him, the rest will come along in its order. The whole faith is important. Many people have one or two doctrines they like and enjoy, but they do not take the whole faith. They are living in a one- or two-room cabin when they might be living in a many-roomed palace. By the time some of these people who call themselves "liberal" have got through watering down the faith, there isn't much left but a vague belief in a deity and a little bundle of moral principles. That is *not* the Christian religion. The faith of the Christian religion is embodied in the Creeds. But you may have to work at those points one at a time, and not be able to take them all at once. You begin with "faith" and move on as you grow and know more to understanding and accepting "the faith."

We said a moment ago "begin with faith in Christ." What do we believe about Christ? Well, I for one believe that He was and is God come in the flesh. I believe that everything in God that can mean anything to us human beings was revealed in Him. But I did not always believe that much. Many another Christian that I know could not have begun there—he had to begin where he could. He might only be able to say that he thought Jesus was the best Man that ever lived, and he admired His character more than anyone else's he ever knew and thought He had done more good for the world. All right, start there. Don't begin with what you *don't* believe; begin with what you *do* believe. You believe Jesus was the best Man that ever lived. Then you are perfectly safe in trying to live as nearly as possible the way He lived. You hear Him say, "Be ye therefore perfect, even as your Father which is in heaven is perfect." You find that is easy to say, and very hard to do. You hear Jesus say, "Love your enemies," and "Do good to them that hate you," and the more you try to do these things, the more impossible do they become.

Then one day you run across a verse that throws light on all this. Jesus says, "Without me, ye can do nothing." Your own moral strength is not enough: you need help from Him, help from on high. You need to pray. His help in prayer, His grace through the Bible and the Church, give you a strength you never had before. You find that the heart of the Christian experience is not trying to imitate Christ, but rather it is calling on Him for help. It is not something you do for Him, it is something He does for you. That takes a lot of the self-effort out of it. You see, if we try to do this Christian business in our own strength, one of two things happens: when we succeed, we get puffed up; and when we fail, we get "sunk." Whereas when we let Christ help us with it, when we succeed, we become grateful; and when we fail, we become penitent. Faith in Christ means that we turn ourselves over to Him so that all this can happen.

70

How does anyone turn himself over to Christ? It is not an emotional upheaval, it is a decision of the will. We consider our whole selves: sins, talents, hopes, fears, aspirations, potentialities—and we bring them to Christ for forgiveness or redirection. When a man asks a woman to marry him, and she accepts him, it is a decision, a life-decision of the most tremendous importance. It is so with the decision about Christ. We surrender as much of ourselves as we can to as much of Christ as we understand. The chief element here is that of decision and commitment. I am shocked to find how many people in our churches have never anywhere made a decisive Christian commitment. They oozed into church membership on a conventional kind of basis, but no one has ever effectively dealt with them spiritually, or helped them make a Christian decision. Such work cannot be done en masse; it must be done individually. There is a vast leakage in our churches, people joining them after proper instruction but then somehow filtering away, like a stream losing itself in a marsh. We shake our heads and wonder what is the matter. But the matter is not far to seek: they should, in most cases, have been converted before they were taken in. (I say in most cases, because at times people get converted after they have come into the church, and we must not try to box the Holy Spirit.) What troubles me is the thousands, yes, tens of thousands, in our churches who have never been converted at all, and who, traveling at their present rate, never will be. People need intense individual attention. The reward in the ministry of working with individuals will convince any clergyman that you cannot do this in crowds. You can preach to crowds, you can teach crowds, you can initiate the idea of conversion in crowds, and make crowds of people hungry for it. But it is like medicine: you can lecture on hygiene to a mass of people, but when you are sick, you want the doctor to give you individual time, punch you and find out where it hurts, diagnose your situation and give the adequate remedy.

We begin the actual Christian experience when we surrender as much of ourselves as we can to as much of Christ as we understand. That is an honest, scientific approach. You do not say you believe something you don't believe. You begin positively where you are. You may not know too much about yourself, but you recognize your sin and need, the need to be different, very different, and your inability to change yourself. Christ may still be only the Best that you know. All right— begin there. Make an act of self-surrender. Do this with another if it will help rivet it, and it very likely will. But make it. Gather up your sins and needs, put them together, bring them to Him for forgiveness and help. Commit yourself to Him in an act of dedication. This act centers in the will, not the emotions. Its reality is not to be determined by whether you see any stars or bright lights, or feel a tingle along your spine; you may and you may not—it is not important. What is important is that you *let go*, let go of your sins and your fears and your inhibitions. Do not look for emotional proof, look for practical proof by the presence in your life of new power, new integration, new joy, new love for people. Jesus Christ has made the first move toward you. He has made the promises, "Him that cometh to me I will in no wise cast out," "Behold, I stand at the door and knock. If any man will open unto me, I will come in. . . ." That is His promise. You do not need to go out and take Him by the arm and pull Him in. You need only to open the door, wide, and invite Him, and He will come in. That is His promise, and its fulfillment is the experience of millions who now know Him as their Lord and Saviour.

Time was when I thought conversion was something for the very good or the very bad, and as I wasn't either, I wasn't a very good subject for it. I had been brought up in the Church, and I do not remember when I was not going into the ministry. Is that conversion? Not necessarily. I thought very good people, like St. Francis, got converted—or very bad people like St. Augustine in his early days. Present-day saints may have been converted, but I really thought they were probably always like that.

And then drunks in the back streets needed it. But why good church-people? I'll tell you why. The test of a man's conversion is whether he has enough Christianity to get it over to other people. If he hasn't, there is something wrong in it. I could not do that. I began lay-reading when I was seventeen. I used to have a small summer congregation for whom I held services. Two or three men in that group met tragic experiences. Why? Partly because what I gave them was so general. There was no conversion in it. I could not get it across. I was like a Scotch friend of mine who said that while his friends could not make him drunk, he couldn't make them sober! There was a recurrent pattern of failure—at those services, and working in army camps during the First World War. Individuals were seeking spiritual help, and I could not give it to them. Their faces still haunt me. I went out to China to teach in a school in old Peking. Again, men were seeking. I should have failed them in the same way, but out there I met a man who challenged me as to whether I had ever made a full commitment of my life to Jesus Christ. He held me to it till I did it. And the very next day a Chinese businessman made his Christian decision with me. Test yourself by this: Can I get across to other people what I believe about Jesus Christ? If not, what real good am I to them, and what real good am I to Him?

There are those who associate conversion with wild religious excitement. They have had enough of that in their time. Some of them seek dignified and formal churches to get away from all that. So far as goes the refusal to be intellectually honest, so far as goes identifying conversion with mere emotional arousal, so far as goes the search for a Church which holds to some objective verities and not merely a lot of subjective feelings, this may be well and good. But let us be careful we do not throw out the baby with the bath water. Real religion never runs on worn tracks. Unless it makes a profound difference in life, we may be only playing with the echoes and counterfeits of it, not the real and original thing. What I should like to see, for people in my own church, is as definite spiritual conversion as the Methodists and Baptists talk about, and then these people helped and trained and brought into the Church by the ancient apostolic rite of Confirmation. But there is something else I should like to see. Some people have had a definite conversion, something that shook and changed them profoundly. Then they came into the Church, and all this was cooled off. Beginning as potential disciples with fire in their hearts, they get turned into church members who just go to church and pay their subscriptions and work on a committee or two, and that is all they do. That is not all the early Church did, and if it had been, you and

I would not be thinking of becoming Christians today. Somebody said you mustn't put a live chick under a dead hen. It bothers me how many Christians begin by being alive, and then get cooled down, not by losing all contact with religious life, but by being exposed to such an anemic form of it that it makes little difference to themselves or others. There is just not much religion behind those blank, lackluster eyes, that necessity to be dragged to church, that grudging gift of perhaps one-half of one per cent of their income. Let us seek conversion, till we find it. There is grave spiritual danger in not asking whether one has ever been converted, or in not pursuing conversion until it takes place. The danger is that this *laissez faire* and procrastination will give such hostages to compromise, and so accustom us to the state of not being converted, that our souls will never spread their wings and rise above the half measures and actual defeats of our unconverted state. Many of us think that conversion is a process that is going on: we come to find that the process has not so much as ever started. We are like people sitting in a railway station, and because there are shouts of stations and times of trains leaving, we think we must be on one of them going somewhere, when actually we are just sitting about in the waiting room. It has never begun at all!

How about the matter of gradualness and suddenness

in conversion? Those who want conversion to be gradual compare it to growth. I would like to remind them that growth *begins* suddenly. It begins when the seed goes in the ground and begins both to die and to live in a new way, at the same time. There is the long period of gradual growth, but that does not take place except it be initiated somewhere. Our birth into the new life is like our birth into natural life. There is the long period of growth within the body of the mother: but conception is sudden, and birth is sudden. The idea that you are not converted, and ought to be, may come to you in a flash. It may germinate in your mind till it comes later to actual rebirth. Many people cover up their spiritual powerlessness, their unsurrendered, unconverted condition, by saying they love the quiet, steady nurture of the Episcopal Church; it isn't always taking them to a fire, or questioning whether they are converted or not. Yes, unhappily that is often true. And that is part of what keeps the Episcopal Church, rich beyond almost all others in so many ways, from being the kind of spiritual force in the world that it ought to be. If anyone can speak for our Communion, it is the late Archbishop William Temple. And this is what he has to say about conversion: "At first or last there must be a sharp break, a conversion or new birth or else there must be a series of conversions, but there is need for real discontinuity.

Often indeed a particular conversion takes a long time and is effective through a gradual process; yet even then its completion takes place at a moment, and though the transition effected in that moment may be very small yet it is in its essential nature abrupt." If you ask what is that moment, I say unhesitatingly it is the moment of self-surrender. When we want God's way more than our own, when we open ourselves to His divine invasion, He comes in, and the transaction is completed. William James said, "The crisis of self-surrender has always been and must always be regarded as the vital turning-point of the religious life."

What does a true conversion involve? Four things, I should say.

First, a break with conscious sin, as far as we can be aware of it. Nearly every one of us knows one or two or five besetting sins that dog us always. There is perhaps a resentment that must be given up. Or there is a wrong relation that must be cleaned up. Or there is a personal plan for our lives which we have never been willing to submit to God. Or there is some lie we are living or repeating. Or there is some kind of self-importance which brings everything back to its relation to us. Someone once said we take hold of God by the handle of our sins. When we let Him come in fully, He takes over those unyielded areas where self has reigned before. A young

fellow was converted not long ago. The conversion re-
volved around letting God have the problem of his
nerves, his fears about support for the future (he had
practically no human means of support), and his relation
to girls. They were specific, concrete. He handed them
to God, as you would pay out three one-dollar bills to a
man to whom you owed them. Because the conversion
was concrete, it meant something, and it stuck.

Second, a provision for adequate time to be given to
God daily. When a child is born, it needs nourishment
at once and from then on. You will need at least twenty
minutes to half an hour in the morning. The mind is
fresher then, and a good period of prayer with God
before the day begins insures a different kind of day.
You will need a Bible, and some plan by which to read
it. You will need some great devotional books to help
you and some great experimental books about prayer,
like those of Dr. Frank Laubach. But you will have to
learn to say your own prayers, too, for no books cover
everything in your daily life, and all needs praying for.

Third, fellowship with other Christians. You are born
into a human family, and you are born again into a
spiritual family. That family is the Church. A member of
a family who never stays home, and only occasionally
sends a small check, is not much of a family member.
You need the sustenance of the family food and the

family caring and the family responsibility. Many think they can break off a piece of faith and continue it by themselves: but they have not yet learned what Christianity is. There is no such thing as Christianity apart from the life of the Church. The spiritual life of people who try to do it all by themselves is as unnatural as a plant that grows up somewhere under a porch, or in a cellar: it is spindly and yellow and misshapen because it has not grown in the sun, as healthy plants grow.

Fourth, we must begin giving away what we have, or we shall lose it. One of the first impulses after we hear a good story is to find someone to tell it to. And one of the first impulses after we have had a real Christian experience is to want to impart it to others. These people who say that their religion is too personal to talk about seem to me to have so little of it they haven't got much to talk about. Falling in love is very personal, too, but did you ever see a youngster in love who didn't want to tell you about his or her beloved? Communists make a hundred million more Communists a year. Do you think your kind of religion is enough to stand up against that? The Christians in a free world have got a tremendous job of persuading to do, if we are going to keep the world free.

Visiting one of our great eastern universities some months ago, I met a young freshman, blue-eyed, healthy, but going through a bad patch because his girl had just thrown him over. I told him I was very sympathetic, but I believed if he could turn his disappointment over to God, and surrender it, God might be able to help him find the meaning of it, and help him to use it in understanding other people in trouble. He wanted to do this, and we had some prayer about it together. Next day he was in again, looking like a different person. He had really surrendered his sorrow and loss, and God had given him peace. Listen to this letter from him: "I wish I could put down in writing everything that is in my heart, but that is sort of impossible. Consequently you will have to read a little into what I say. Ever since that wonderful day when we were together, my life has become a sort of a picture that is constantly unfolding to me. Now I can see where I am, and, I think, where I am going. I am really and seriously thinking of becoming a minister. Whereas before I had too many interests in a life's work, now there is just one. The more I think about it, the more it seems to fit in with what I want and feel. Perhaps this can show you how deep this wonderful thing has gone with me. Going to church now really means something. It is hard to see how I remained cold to it in the past. The same thing has applied to the Bible. Every night when I read a little out of it, it gives me a feeling of grasping something concrete as well as spiritual. Tonight I started reading *The Greatest Story Ever Told.* God brought this book to me which I can really understand and appreciate. At last the answers to my questions about Jesus are beginning to come. With each page I realize more and more what a tremendous story of strength and good surrounds Him. This is truly the start of my Christian education. . . . I feel a great benevolence toward the people around me, a desire to share with them what I have found. Several times within the last few weeks I have had very gratifying talks with others on what has happened to me. It was amazing to see the old fumbling, reticent person I used to be, talking freely and saying what he meant. Words won't convey how grateful I am." He is a student in one of the most corrosively irreligious universities on this continent. The education he was getting did not help him to meet life. His Christian conversion did. The conversion happened in connection with the thing that humanly meant most to him, namely, the loss of his fiancée. God came to him right at the point of his need. He always does.

5

THE FELLOWSHIP OF THE CHURCH

When a man becomes a Christian, he soon finds himself confronted with two things with which he must reckon all the rest of his days. One is the Bible, which is the Book that tells what Christianity is, beginning at the beginning when it was at its purest, and therefore provides an everlasting test and means of toning up our present-day Christianity to accord more fully with the original. The second is the Church, the company of those who believe in Jesus Christ, belong to His Society, want to live as He lived, and to build His Kingdom in the world. Taken as a whole, Protestant Christianity has emphasized the Bible as over against the Church, and Catholic Christianity has emphasized the Church as over against the Bible. A Church which is both Evangelical and Catholic, like the Episcopal Church, emphasizes both, and believes that without either you have only a partial and one-sided view of the Christian religion.

There are at least five reasons why the Church is essential.

The first is that Jesus founded it. His work in the world was in part an attempt to reform and revitalize the religion of His people the Jews. Their religion, with its original impulses in pure spiritual power, had in many places sunk down to an organization that was corrupt politically, split hairs about moral ideals, and released very little genuine spiritual power. Jesus knew enough about human nature to know that He was risking creating something that might go in this exact same direction. In many places it has done so.

Ray Stannard Baker says that Lincoln Steffens once told him a parable. "One day," he said, "Satan and I were walking down Fifth Avenue together, when we saw a man stop suddenly and pick a piece of Living Truth right out of the air."

"Doesn't that worry you?" Steffens asked Satan. "Don't you know it is enough to destroy you?"

"Yes," said Satan, "but I'm not worried. That's a beautiful truth now, but the man who caught it will name it, and then he will organize it, and by that time it will be dead. If he would let it live, and live it, it would destroy me. No, I'm not worried."

Jesus wanted to "live it and let it live," and He wanted His people to do the same thing. He wanted the Church to be "spiritual," in the real and not the sentimental sense. But Jesus was realistic. He knew that there is no such thing in this world as spirit without body. The spirit of a man is more important than his body: it may remain strong long after his body is weak or sick or old, and we believe it will survive when that body is dead. But in this world, we find the two together. The spirit wears the body. The body is infused by the spirit. Jesus' company would have to recognize that. The spirit of the Church is more important than the body, for the spirit of the Church is the Holy Spirit. But it must be a spirit within an institution. Jesus did not set in motion a purely "spiritual" religion. From the very first when people came in contact with Him, they came in contact also with His people, with the company of those who moved about Him. The apostles were called very early in the story, and thereafter you never find Him without them.

The second reason why the Church is essential concerns the nature of Christianity itself. We have used the symbol of birth, and said that entering on the Christian experience was like a new birth. But we are always born, not only into life and the world, but into a family. The family is the organic unit. It exists partly to produce more births. Now the Church is Christ's big family. It is broken up into parishes and local churches, which correspond to individual homes. A home is an organic thing. It is not primarily a house, with a cellar and kitchen and living room and bedrooms—the house is just the outside of a home. But you do not find very many homes without houses. The essence of Christianity is this family relationship. God is our Father, and we gather as His children in the home of the Church. From the first, Christians have been incorporated into the body of the Church.

Now there are a great many people abroad today who have a very erroneous notion about what Christianity is. They think being a Christian is trying to live like Christ, following the Golden Rule and the Sermon on the Mount. That is all fine. But imagine telling a two-day-old baby that his job is to learn and live up to all the family ideals! The first thing he needs is milk. He needs love, attention and care. It will be a long while before he has grown up in the family and can even begin to carry out the family heritage. But he is a member of the family the day he is born! Christ did not so much set in motion new teachings; you can find almost everything He said in some form or other in the Jewish and other religions. What He *did* do was to set in motion a movement which is a family. From the first, Christians have been not so much people who believe in His teaching as people who belong to His family and His movement. It is at once both a simpler thing than just accepting His teaching, and a harder one: simpler, because in a way you are carried along in the movement of the Church; harder, because you become involved at once in human relations where you are meant to reflect the spirit of Christ. Anybody who thinks he can just dip into the New Testament and pick up a piece of morality and go off and live it out on his own, has no idea what the Christian religion is. That may be *his* idea of what Christianity is; but it is not the New Testament's idea, nor the idea of the body of Christ from the first day until now.

A third reason why the Church is essential is that Christianity is out to bring all life under its sway. Christianity is a kind of free and voluntary totalitarianism: it wants to see the rule of God in every area of human existence. Much of life is material and physical. We need a growing movement that captures the loyalties of more and more people, more and more communities, more and more nations. We must hold the ground we take, and train the people we win. They in turn are meant to win others. You cannot think of any movement's capturing the world without making use of organizations and institutions. All of life's materials, all of life's institutions, are meant to become as sacraments for God's power. Something must give a lead in all this. As Christians we follow our Lord when He took bread and broke it and called it His Body; and wine and called it His Blood. Through that Sacrament He comes to His people with grace and forgiveness and power; but through it He also symbolizes to us the sacramental nature of all life and all material things. Not bread and wine only, but all things—business, industry, commerce, politics, education—are likewise meant to be symbols and sacraments. The Church has to keep this ideal of the sacramentalizing of all life before humanity, and lead them in how it is done.

A fourth reason why the Church is essential is that we personally need it. Many a time have I seen people start off in a quite individualistic way on a Christian experience, only to find that they could not go it alone. We need the warmth and inspiration of others who are foraging and discovering in this whole area. We help them up when they are down, they help us up when we are down. The interplay of Christian love and service within the family of Christ trains us for love and service toward those outside that family, and these draw them into that family. We must continually be reminded of the richness of the Church, the varied and various people who compose it. We may not think we like some of them: no matter—we shall come to like them when we are truly converted; but they are our brothers, as blood brothers are, whether we like them or not. Sometimes we look with scorn at the Church and do not want to belong to it. We say there are too many hypocrites in it: the answer to which is, "Come on in, there is always room for one more!" Or the much deeper answer, that on its human side the Church is not a museum but a school or even a hospital, not a place where people are on exhibition or parade, but a place where they are learning how to live. They haven't arrived—they are traveling, we hope in the right direction. But the Church on its divine side is a source of spiritual power, and we go back to it when we need a refill.

There is a story about a man who sat in front of a fire talking with his minister. He said to him, "Parson, I don't think I'll come to church any more. Religion is a very personal thing. I think I'll just try to work it out by myself." The parson said nothing, but took a pair of tongs and lifted a live coal out of the fire, and laid it on the hearth. They both watched it slowly go out. Then the man said, "I see what you mean. I'll be back next Sunday."

A fifth reason why the Church is essential is that we cannot hope to win against the forces of evil in this world fighting singly and solo. Light is up against darkness: do you think your little single candle is enough to rout it? One light or two or a hundred will not do it, but the lights from a whole city will light a night sky, and you can see the glow for miles. The old, eternal power of evil is always here; but in the past couple of generations this power has created for itself an engine of force and persuasion in the world such as mankind has never known.

Communism is the "church" of evil and slavery: it is a missionary church dedicated to winning the world for atheism and tyranny and materialism. Man has never seen such ingenious devilry before, nor so well organized. A Christian here or there has little power against it. The massed force of Christians everywhere is the one thing Communism fears. That is why it seeks to throttle the Church first of all wherever it goes. If it leaves the Church to function at all, it makes sure the Church does not function by criticizing the state. Its teeth are drawn. Surely no individualistic religion can hope to cope with such colossal evil. When people talk about having "their own religion," you may be sure they are apart from the stream of the historic Church, often sentimental and complacent, and have never even contemplated the real task of religion on earth, which is to deliver man from sin and evil, in himself and in his oppressors. Do you think a little individualistic religion can hope to stand up against the forces of evil that are loose in the world today? If so, you are doing a lot of unrealistic wishful thinking. It needs us all, standing shoulder to shoulder, all believers in God, all believers in man, all believers in freedom, all churches side by side: nothing less can hope to win.

Let us go back for a little and have a look at the early Church. Some of its people had seen Jesus in the flesh;

some had not. There were ex-Jews among them and ex-pagans. There were rich and poor. They were both withdrawn from the world and very much in it. They were withdrawn from its cruelties and impurities and idolatries, but they were in it as a challenge and a leaven. Let us remember that that little scratch company of men and women were the human instruments of a force that superseded both Judaism and paganism. It must have been a close-knit, determined group, with very close association between their Leader and themselves, and amongst themselves. Presumably most of them stayed in their own kind of business, but the center of their lives was the Risen Christ and His company of believers. Dr. E. F. Scott, in his book *The Nature of the Early Church*, says of them, "In the few glimpses we have of them they are always together, in prayer, in the study of the Scriptures, at the common meal. As in Jesus' lifetime they are not merely a number of persons who believe in Jesus and look for His return, but 'the brethren.'"

As time went on, the Church inevitably became a more definite entity, with customs and regulations, above all with a liturgical procedure, especially for the Church's central service—the celebration of the Holy Communion. The Church was bound to take on outward forms which both suggest and channel inner realities. There must be an outward side to the Church's life, as there is to the life of a family. Form is no contradiction to reality. If you feel a warm friendliness toward another person, it is good to be able to put out your hand to him, or to smile at him, in gesture of the friendliness you feel. Churches with no form usually wind up with a characteristic simplicity which in turn becomes itself a kind of form. You can see this necessary, inevitable, and rightful kind of formality coming into the life of the early Church. It was not a rival or enemy of reality, it was a way of expressing reality.

The great central realities of the Church's worship were the preaching of the Word and the bringing of the Sacraments to the people. The Sacrament of initiation was Holy Baptism: when anyone became a Christian, he or she was baptized in the name of Jesus Christ.* And after confirmation by one of the apostles, or their successors, being informed and mature Christians, people received the Sacrament of Holy Communion. That was the Sacrament of sustenance, of continuation. Some people think that the preaching of the Word is the whole of the Gospel. It is a very important part, and by it people usually come to faith. "Faith cometh by hearing, and hearing by the Word of God." † But, as Baptism is the outward sign that corresponds to the beginnings of

* Acts 2:38.
† Romans 10:17.

92

Christian experience in conversion, so Holy Communion is the outward sign that corresponds to the continuation of the Christian experience in nurture and growth. The Holy Communion is the steady food of Christians. This outward side of the Church is necessary because life is as it is. You send presents in packages to protect them. Trees have bark because sap cannot run without a protective covering. Water comes into our houses in pipes, because it would be of no use to us in a stream without a channel. People who think they can just be "spiritual," without regard for the outward forms and worship of the Church, are fooling themselves by their own pride of self-sufficiency, and they are failing to remember the very nature of Christianity itself. We need the inward, and we need the outward. We need the Spirit, but we need also the body.

Now side by side with these formal and liturgical services there went also informal gatherings which have always been an intrinsic part of the Christian life in the world. The late Dom Gregory Dix, in his monumental book *The Shape of the Liturgy*, says that in the early Church there were the Eucharist and the "synaxis" or "syneleusis," which he calls the "non-eucharistic 'general meeting' of the whole local church." This might correspond to our ordinary Sunday morning services where the Holy Communion is not celebrated, or it might correspond to another kind of gathering which has been part of the life of the Church from the first. It says in Acts 2:42, "They continued in the apostles' doctrine and in the fellowship and in the breaking of bread and in prayers." The New Testament word for "church" is "ecclesia," the called-out. But this word "fellowship" in Greek is "koinonia." This fellowship was not another thing than the Church, but it was the state of being in fellowship with one another in the Church. Such fellowship is expressed, not only when you meet with other Christians at formal worship, with your eyes on the Cross and the altar and your mind on God and our Lord and the Gospel, but also when you meet with other Christians in informal gatherings, with your eyes looking into the eyes of the others and your mind on their needs and their grace. Such informal gatherings have been part of the life of the Church in every age, contributing to the life of the great organized Church, and drawing itself from that life. There are and will always be many who will not understand what the big, formal, institutional Church is about, unless they discover the Church in the smaller manifestation of it, the more informal and spontaneous, where the Presence of Christ is written on men's faces and His reality there with them in the way they greet and meet with each other.

Today, in uncounted places, men and women, sometimes together, more often meeting separately, gather in some stated place, say once a week, to open their minds and hearts to one another, to wait upon God, to see what the Holy Spirit does to and through human relationships centered in Christ, to hear the Scriptures and to comment on them, to pray and fall silent together, to exchange spiritual experience, to bring out problems and concerns, to find God's answers being wrought out in fellowship, and to go away strangely uplifted and refreshed. It is a different kind of uplifting and refreshing from that which may come from preaching or evangelistic services or sacramental ones. There is no pressure of other men without, more of the quiet working of God within. They will sometimes feel such a common stirring that it is as if a current of power were being passed through the company. I do not wonder that at Pentecost they experienced "the sound as of a rushing mighty wind, and it filled all the house where they were sitting." * A current of wind, blowing upon all, bringing quiet power with it, is just what this resembles most. Thomas Kelly says truly that this experience defies precise description. Neither can you always guarantee the Spirit's Presence and power—He, not we, decides when and how and whether He will come. But He often does come when we fulfill the conditions. We are carried out beyond ourselves in

* Acts 2:2.

this experience, we are acted upon without coercion, and we act ourselves without self-effort. It is as if a heavenly spiritual stream began to flow in which differences become only enrichments and not divisions, and in which we are carried along into new discoveries. In an honest, waiting, listening, silent company, God often comes. There are people who have made studies of "group dynamics," and these are good if they help toward more experience of group fellowship; but I submit that no one knows the real power of a group who does not know also the Holy Spirit, who seems to find His most natural entering place and home in this world, not in individual hearts, but in companies. Obviously a small company is easier to infuse than a large one. Obviously a parish, say of five hundred people, would be immeasurably deepened and fortified if a considerable number of its people met every week in such small companies as this. Nowhere else in the world does one find such a combination of being acted upon from without, yet of such spontaneity from within.

Here in such a company many a person has first learned what spiritual power is, first seen what a difference and what kind of difference Jesus Christ makes in the lives of people, first learns the real experience of "common prayer" which is not necessarily generated because all pray out of the same book, and first begins to see how Christians may be the seed of a new order of society. Here in such a company people often feel free to be themselves, as they do not have any opportunity to be in a formal service, and as most churches make no provision for them to be at all. The very wearing of "Sunday clothes" becomes a symbol of a kind of unreality and stuffiness: where shall these people see one another in their shirt sleeves, where be able to ventilate their real doubts, get their real questions answered, and develop some genuine fellowship relations with their other Christian brethren? Here, too, many take the first steps in religious articulation, giving account of the faith and experience that is in them, in which most of our more educated churches are so lamentably weak. The emotional groups and sects teach a kind of articulation, but it is often so rigid with doctrine, so little mixed with humor and naturalness, that it is more likely to put people off than to win them. Our educated communions, fearing mistakes and excesses, instead of finding a way of doing it better, and teaching their lay people how to do it, abandon the whole thing, decide not to do it at all, and let the ministers do all their articulation for them.

Of course, the articulation in such a gathering is utterly different from making a speech. It is a matter of sensing with delicate discernment just where the whole group is at the moment, so that one's words are relevant, and in what direction the Holy Spirit wants the group to move next. One does not so much speak "to" as speak "for" the company. It must be spontaneous, almost ruminative, as if one were thinking aloud. The very suggestion of a "speech" will kill it. One speaks in a quieter tone. Henry D. Thoreau said, "There are many fine things which we cannot say if we have to shout." Here is required a greater dedication to God, and a greater sensitiveness to people, than we often experience. Speech is punctuated by living silences in which the Spirit of God can work.

Small companies like this are growing up rapidly all over the world. They are one of the "signs of hope" which Dr. Elton Trueblood notes in his book of that name. In reviewing a little booklet called *Creating Christian Cells*, Dr. Chad Walsh says, "The cell is the missing link between Sunday church services, which of necessity are general in nature, and the private religious life of the individual. Such groups are coming into being in the most unlikely places and generating new religious vitality." There is nothing which our church people need more, there is no better way of exposing the unchurched to the Christian life and message, and there is no kind of meeting our clergy need more to learn how to create and to conduct. Our seminaries ought to teach men how this is done. Nothing would help them in the other parts of their ministry more than to learn the delicate art of leading, yet not over-leading, the small company of the "koinonia."

One such group began when a minister went down one day into the boiler room of the church and said to the sexton, "Herbie, are you in spiritual power?" Both these men were Christians, but not much was happening to or through them. "No," said Herbie honestly and somewhat wistfully, "are you?" The minister said he was not. When we are not in spiritual power, it means we are not really in touch with God, so that He can neither come fully to us nor get through us to others. The two men sat down and began to be honest with each other about where they were actually falling down in their Christian commitment—resentments, fear, dishonesty, low-level thoughts; and when they were through they got on their knees together and asked God for forgiveness and received it. It was good. It was like a spiritual bath. They said, "Let's do this again." They met again the next week. They began to meet every week. They asked two other men to join them after praying about who they should be. Then others came. This became the nucleus of a group that has been prolific in individual conversions, and in the formation of other cells that have broken off from it and taken root elsewhere. Scores of them can be traced. Have we ever thought that *this* might be the way to keep making new Christians, instead of by membership drives and various kinds of super-heated special efforts? This ought to be the constant work of the Church, by which there are "daily added unto the church such as should be saved." *

On one university campus, two undergraduates who had had a Christian experience through their summer vacation felt led to set in motion some cell groups in that university. They talked with the religious authorities and were given a "green light" on it. They went to work with their friends one by one, and that year eighteen cell groups sprang up on that campus. The next year there were forty, and the year after about seventy. Individuals from that university have gone to speak to small groups in other universities, taking the leaven of this kind of dynamic faith with them and setting it to work in other places. In one university where this work only began less than two years ago, there are more than a hundred and fifty men in such groups. It is as if at a certain point the human soul becomes so warm with faith that, fanned by the Spirit of God, it bursts into flame, and that flame sets other souls alight.

This appears to be the characteristic way in which the Holy Spirit is awakening the Church and reaching out into the world of our time. Such groups began in the early Church, have continued side by side with the insti-

* Acts 2:47.

tutional and organized Church, and are the most fresh and contemporaneous way for people to come into touch with Christ and His life through the Church today. As clergy and people learn something of what the deeper meaning of the Church is, get more and more converted themselves, two things happen: (1) the old ways and customs and services of the Church take on fresh meaning and significance and reality; and (2) power comes into the life of the Church from the Holy Spirit. Here is found the hope of a reawakened Church and a redeemed world.

6

SOURCES OF POWER

Whenever anyone comes into a vital Christian experience which makes a dent and a difference in his life, the question immediately arises: Will this be an emotional incident, or will he keep going in this new life? The answer depends upon whether he keeps growing through the use of the sources of power that are available for Christians to use. You remember the story of the boy who fell out of bed, and next morning his mother asked him how it happened; and he said, "I guess I went to sleep too close to the place where I got in." We want awakening, and we want to stay awakened. How shall we do it?

There are six sources of power that are available to us all. If rightly used, they are bound to result in a sustained and growing and vigorous Christian life.

The first is *prayer*. I suppose that all people pray at some time. When we get in a jam, we ask for help from anywhere we think we may find it. There was a soldier on Okinawa who prayed, "O God, You know I have asked You for a lot of things I didn't need, and said a lot of things I didn't mean. But now I'm not foolin'!" Everybody prays that way. Because it is often a matter of "Gimme, gimme," self-centered and childish, God must deal with it as we deal with a selfish child's request. But when we are converted, when we turn over our lives to Christ so far as we can, the avenue of mature prayer is opened up. Conversion is, among other things, going into business with God. Through it we become concerned not so much about what we want as about what He wants. And when that happens, we begin really to pray. I think the other kind of elementary, frightened, selfish prayer may be real, too, but we forsake it after a while for genuine, mature, unselfish Christian prayer.

The art of Christian prayer seems to lie in strong, unselfish desire, and the readiness to relinquish the desire. When Jesus prayed in Gethsemane, He said, "Father, if it be possible, let this cup pass from me. Nevertheless not My will but Thine be done." The prospect of death must have affected Him as it would us, yet He would confront it if this were the Father's will for Him. He could pray asking that it be spared Him, He could pray saying He would meet it if God willed it. Most of us pray only with desire, we do not pray with the relinquishment of desire. We do not do this because we fear God will not do what we want, will not answer. He may not do what we want, but He always answers. Who would say that God did not answer Jesus' prayer in Gethsemane? How many of us know that sometimes God answers Yes, sometimes He answers No, and sometimes He answers Not yet! But He always answers, as you always answer your child's request if you love him. You give what is best.

If you say, Then why ask?, Jesus anticipated your question. He said, "Your heavenly Father knoweth that ye have need of all these things." Prayer is a mysterious share in creation and redemption. There seem to be blessings and power and healing and guidance and the joining of circumstances in what we call "coincidences" which only prayer helps God to release. I do not know why this is: I am convinced *that* it is. William Temple said many wise things, but never a wiser than when he said, "When I pray for people coincidences happen. And when I stop praying the coincidences stop." That is literally true from my experience and that of thousands of others. Prayer puts you in the stream of God's life and power. It brings again the freshness of the hour of conversion. It reaches into things that were not then included and brings them under His sway. It sets loose in me, and I am convinced in others, the flowing of the power and compassion of God.

What, then, should we do about prayer? Three things I suggest: (1) Set apart a time each morning, half an hour if possible. Give that time regularly to God till it becomes as habitual as your breakfast at a regular hour, so that you miss it when you don't have it. It had better be before the mail and paper arrive and the telephone begins. Choose a place where you can be alone, probably your own room unless your house is small and crowded, in which case you may find it good to drop into an open church on your way to work. You need, for an effective early morning time of devotion, a Bible; some book to set your prayers in motion, like John Baillie's *Diary of Private Prayer*, or E. Herman's *Creative Prayer*, or one of Frank Laubach's or Stanley Jones' or Evelyn Underhill's books; and some kind of notebook in which to jot down the thoughts that come to you when you pray and listen, so that you do not forget them: there may be nuggets of God's direction in them. (2) Cultivate the habit of praying as often as you can think of it. You have a moment in the office when you are free: spend it praying for someone. You are lying awake at night and cannot sleep—wonderful time for a good long prayer for many people. You are walking down the street alone; your thoughts can be idle or wayward, or they can be turned into prayers. Talking with God becomes natural after we know Him and begin to love Him. It is amazing what life takes on of meaning, significance, excitement, when we begin working with Him, and that is what prayer really is. (3) As soon as possible, get with some other people who can pray with you. Jesus' promise concerned where "two or more of you be agreed." Great power is generated and released by common prayer. You may be a little self-conscious at first—all of us have been, but that can be surmounted as we confess it laughingly and get on to the main business. Women are particularly adept at this and become great channels of power by it. I know a group of them that meets once a week for prayer and fellowship. In winter when the roads are difficult they sometimes meet over the telephone. Everybody would be stronger for learning to pray with other people.

The second source of power is *worship*. Just "going to church" can be of little significance; but the worship of God is never insignificant. A group of people confessing their common sins, asking for their common necessities, thanking God for their common blessings, lifting up their hearts in common praise and worship through prayers and hymns is a wonderful company to be in. Jesus wants us to worship God "in spirit and in truth." He says God is seeking people who do that. Why, I wonder? Do you think God wants us to fawn and prostrate ourselves and bootlick Him? I don't. But I think God wants us to "get the news" about Him, and know something of His wonder and glory and majesty. And our worship is just our acknowledgment of these things in the only way we can acknowledge them and respond to them. Worhip is our expression to God of our love for Him. When we really love people, we tell them so. That is our right and natural response to them. When we really love God, we say and sing praises to Him. That is our right and natural response to Him.

If sincerity and reality are the essentials of worship, why do it in formal and prearranged ways—why not let it pour out spontaneously? It is a very good thing to let it pour out spontaneously sometimes: the silent or vocal worship of God in little companies of Christians in fellowship is very real and very moving worship. But the supreme act of Christian worship is the Holy Communion. From the very beginning the Church has had to choose some form by which this should be celebrated. Its present form corresponds remarkably to the earliest forms known. How terribly far short the service would fall if at each celebration the celebrant had to make up a service of his own for the occasion! There is room for spontaneous expression within our formal services, but as motors run better on roads, and trains on tracks, so public worship seems facilitated by making use of previous experience and by the use of words which become familiar, and can be known and followed by all. Now and then you find a man with a great talent for conducting public worship, but for one of them there are a thousand with no talent at all: they will do better, and help the people to worship more genuinely, if they use the rich and rounded and adequate words that have been used for years, even for centuries, in the worship of God. Hymns do not become unreal by their familiarity, they become more real. Prayers, if they are prayers, and not just words arranged in the form of prayers, are better for being beautiful, balanced, and familiar. But, whether you do it informally or formally, no Christian can get on without the stimulus and constant help of the worship of Almighty God. It seems that in it we are putting out something, but in its effects we shall see that we are receiving from it.

The third source of power is the *Bible*. To hear some people talk, you would think that there was nothing in the Bible but chapters on "begat," and this only shows how little they know of this library of books bound under one cover which we call The Bible. The Old Testament is the record of God's dealing with the nation of the Jewish people, and through it runs an expectation of a Messiah. The New Testament is the declaration that He has come, and the record of His life, His death, His resurrection and ascension, together with the story of the beginnings of the early Church, and some letters, mostly of St. Paul, written to churches in their beginning.

Let me make some suggestions as to where you begin, for many today are where a young man is who is a good member of the church in a fashion, but who told me recently that he had never read a word of the Bible or heard it except when he heard it read in church! It is customary for people to begin with the Gospels, then read the Acts, and then variously turn to the Old Testament or to the Epistles. I think this order for a beginner is wrong. Let us remember that the Epistles were written precisely for the instruction and training of new Christians. Because St. Paul wrote most of them, and because he often used long, involved sentences, and because the King James Version contains many words of archaic English, the Epistles seem like very tough reading to us. I advise you to get a good modern translation, like Moffatt's, or Phillips' translation of the Epistles, called *Letters to Young Churches*, or to get the new Revised Standard Version, which is probably the best, and with the help of a good commentary, like Dummelow or Gore or the Interpreter's Bible, begin to dig in to the Epistles. It was something of a discovery for me, not to read the Epistles in the light of the Four Gospels, but to read the Four Gospels in the light of the Epistles. They are what St. Paul fed young Christians on some twenty-five years after the Resurrection. They are the corrective to the idea that Christianity is mostly ethics. I reread the Epistles recently to get a general, swift impression of them; and this was the impression: The Person for whom the ages have waited has come, and in Him was all the fullness of God Himself. He walked here as a Man, but He was God Incarnate; He died for the sins of the world; He rose again from the dead and ascended into glory; He left His Church to represent Him on earth—in the light of all which people who call themselves by His Name will of course try to behave themselves in His spirit. Over all is the blaze of the Resurrection. All of life is different because of that. Read them for yourself, and let them make on you their own profound impression.

We need to get a balanced diet of the Bible, such as you find in the lectionary in front of the Prayer Book,* or the selections of the Bible-Reading Fellowship. Or we may read consecutively one book in the Old and one in the New Testament. The deeper we go in the Christian life, the more we need and value and love the Bible. And the more we read and know and enjoy and feed on the Bible, the deeper we shall go in the Christian life. They are correlative and cognate. One who keeps making fresh discoveries of Christ for himself will be delightedly surprised to find them somewhere in the pages of the old Book itself, discovered long before by someone else.

The fourth source of power is the *Holy Communion*. The night before His death, Jesus was at supper with His apostles by His own arrangement. There were on the

* Pp. x ff.

table the traditional loaf of bread and bottle of wine. He was mindful that what would take place next day would part Him from them in the mere human sense, and they would never be together again in this same way. Yet His spiritual presence was to be greater and more universal than ever before, and it would be just as real as His physical presence. How should He keep forever reminding His people of this? What could be a continual reminder of Him, of His death for the sins of all men, of His continued life in their midst? It must be something concrete. Instead of a *thing*, He chose an *action*. Whether by premeditated plan or sheer impulse of genius, He took the loaf, broke it apart, and handed it round to them, saying, "This is My Body." And after supper taking the cup, He handed it to them, saying, "This is My Blood." The torn-ness of the loaf, the out-pouredness of the wine made this the perfect symbol, the perfect channel of what He wanted and knew they needed. The Sacrament of Baptism and the Sacrament of Holy Communion were the two Sacraments which He instituted, though there are other rites and acts within the Christian Church which have sacramental meaning and significance.

This has become the central service of Christian worship. From that night until now, in hundreds of different ways and languages, this great sacrificial act has been repeated in accord with His command, "This do ye. . . ."

We find it more than a memorial, for He is there with us in a living way at the Holy Communion. We believe that nothing changes in the material nature of the bread and wine, but that these are infused by His spirit. He puts Himself into them, as one can be said to put himself into a letter. This is not mechanical or magical, it is one of the very great ways He has chosen to come to His people. There, at the Holy Communion, is felt and known a living Presence. Non-Romans do not believe in transubstantiation; neither do Episcopalians believe merely in a memorial feast. The nearest we can come to stating our own position of belief is that in the Holy Communion is found the Real Presence of Christ. When we take that particle of consecrated bread, and drink that sip of consecrated wine, Christ chooses truly to come to us through them.

Unless we are steady and regular in our devotional habits, there is no use in entering upon them at all. Unless our prayers are daily at a fixed time, we shall probably not say them at all. Unless our Bible study is of the same regularity, it will trail off into inaction. Now there are an appalling number of people who have been received into the church and taken upon themselves their mature Christian vows, who come to Holy Communion when it suits their convenience, or who never come at all. Some say it has never been anything but a routine and formality to them—which only means their dedication to Christ is defective, or that they have never made consistent use of the Holy Communion over a long enough period of time to test out its working validity. It is little use to urge people to come to Communion more often, if their hearts have never been deeply touched by Christ—conversion is the real doorway to Communion. But surely something on which Christ Himself laid such stress and on which the historic Church has always laid such stress cannot be a matter of individual option. We are meant to do this thing regularly. We shall never know its power until we do. Will you do one thing—will you promise God and someone else who knows you that, for at least a year, you will make your Communion once a week at the least? I made that rule for myself when I was a school-boy, and I do not break it except in urgent situations. Every Christian ought to make his Communion every Sunday unless there is special reason why he cannot. By openness of heart, and by regularity of attendance, you will learn to depend on this great source of power in sustaining the Christian life. In prayer we reach up to God, in Holy Communion He reaches down to us. There if anywhere we know the "helping Hand of grace."

The fifth source of power is *fellowship*. We have dealt with the matter of the fellowship of the Church. We begin our fellowship usually at a simple, social level, and the Church needs to provide occasions like that for its people. In a great many parishes now, you will find they hold a coffee hour after morning service. There parishioners and new people, old and young, rich and poor, all sorts and kinds, can gather and feel at home and be made welcome. You will meet many who are there because they need fellowship. There is an immense amount of sheer human loneliness in the hearts of all kinds of people today. Sometimes they go to church to see if anybody will attempt to meet them and make friends. You know how often when they come into church it is like stepping into a deep-freeze. No smile, no handshake, no warmth—just a look that says, "Who is this stranger?" We can and should use all kinds of legitimate social occasions just to meet such people and get to know them. Simple friendliness comes first.

Next comes some kind of participation. Find out what people can do, and see how they can put that talent to work for the Church. A businessman friend of mine became a Christian. The first thing I did was to include him on helping to get some money for a radio program I was conducting. He did it well, and it made him feel like a member of the firm. People no longer feel strange or inept or like outsiders when you enlist their help and put their talents to work. There are men and women in all sorts of positions where they can do things for the church, e.g., on newspapers and radio stations and magazines, and everybody is doing something which the Church can help him or her to do better. The more participation we can enlist, the more people will grow.

Then comes the deeper kind of fellowship which many want, all need, and few find. The places where frankly I see new and young Christians growing and going ahead most today are the places where a small group gathers regularly, with the best leadership afforded, and studies, prays, and exchanges ideas until each of them becomes effective in making faith real to other people. Often we need imagination for this, which may be stimulated by others. Often we need courage, and we catch it from others who are really doing it. Often we need to know that others are facing just our kind of difficulties and opportunities, and to learn from them how to do something and how not to do it. Women should be brought together in small groups for prayer which so deepens their spiritual life that they become transmitters of their faith to others by life and by word. Men should be brought together in small groups for exchange of experience and prayer which steadily transforms the life about them. Let half a dozen men or women come together after prayer and the making of spiritual friends with one another, meet steadily, study, work, till they become a kind of team; and you will find a power in the company which is very much more than the sum of the power you find in each individual; "two or three" is the condition for His Presence and power. The Holy Spirit seeks the company to work in and through. Not all will be ready for this deeper kind of experience, but some will, and the Church must change its gears and learn how to provide for this very great need of fellowship at a deeper level for its people. We must get new people doing this—not the dear old pious shopworn Christians that have gone to church for years and done very little real changing inside, but the lively and attractive and imaginative people to whom all this is new, and who bring a fresh breeze with them into the Church. They will probably make some mistakes: these are little beside the big mistake of doing nothing at all. Read what you can on it. *Creating Christian Cells** will help you, I am sure. But there is no substitute for launching out and learning by doing.

This brings me to the last source of power about which I would speak, and that is the use of the *right kind of books*. Until our minds are satisfied about some intellectual matters we shall never be quite easy or sure in the faith. Unless we know something about the history of the Church, and the faith of the Church, we shall be

* To be had from Book Stall, 61 Gramercy Park, North, New York 10, N.Y.

emotional children, without adequate foundations. Unless we dig deep into great books on spiritual consecration, we shall not know how to handle many of the situations that arise, or what our next step in growth ought to be. We have already mentioned three kinds of books: let me take a little longer on each of them.

For those who find themselves caught in a secular existence, conditioned by the completely naturalistic outlook of much modern education, nothing else will help so much as reading the kind of book that helps them see they have faced only a part of reality. Practically all C. S. Lewis' books are written for people whose outlook is irreligious, skeptical, typically modern, for he used to be that kind of person himself and has become a kind of apostle to them. For those troubled by evil in the world of a good God, his *Problem of Pain* is fine. For those who need to see how far off the track much of their thinking is, his satire *The Screwtape Letters* will be entertaining and very illuminating. For those who just believe everything in this universe is all tied up in a box that science can completely explain, there is his great book *Miracles. The Case for Christianity* is also good. He knows how modern skeptics think and feel and he knows how to answer them.

Many think we Christians believe a lot of things we don't believe. They think we believe a lot of things that are piffle, when actually there is good reason for believing in them. They have never found out what the mind of the Church is on the great matters of its own faith. They take two or three things they can believe, and miss all the great richness of the Church's full faith, because they neither know what it is, or why we believe it. For a good exposition of the meaning of the Creeds, I commend *The Faith of the Church*, by Drs. Pike and Pittenger.

Then we need exposure to the kind of books that help set in motion and keep going a dynamic religious experience. Most of Stanley Jones' books are like that: I commend especially *Abundant Living* for beginners in the spiritual life. Dr. Elton Trueblood has written several books, all of which are in this category: *The Predicament of Modern Man*, *Foundations of Reconstruction*, *Signs of Hope*, *The Life We Prize*, and others. Two smaller booklets that will help are *Faith That Works* * and *Here's How*.* Dr. Frank Laubach is one of the world's modern saints, and his *Prayer, the Mightiest Force in the World*, and *Wake Up or Blow Up* give the two sides of his ministry—the deep devotion and the wide service. Books like these are guideposts on the spiritual pilgrimage and

* Published by The Evangel, 61 Gramercy Park North, New York 10, N. Y.

keep us from settling back in what we already know, and being content with what we have already discovered.

Let us then use the "means of grace" provided for us, and turn again and again to the sources of power, where we may initiate or renew our faith. Each one of them is like a well from which we can draw fresh water in our need.

7

HOW SHOULD CHRISTIANS LIVE?

We have tried, thus far, to point out the situation in which we find ourselves, the adequacy of the Person of Christ for human life, our own need of supernatural help, the reality of Christian conversion, and the ways in which we can sustain the Christian life we have begun. We come now to a most important question: How should Christians live? In the light of this much help from above, what kind of people should we be from day to day, in our life, in our homes, in our business, in our relationships?

Because we are hooked and geared to a Power greater than any other in the world, Christians are able to meet the trouble and sorrow and pain of this world with victory. There are those, I know, who believe that faith ought to be a kind of guarantee against trouble. If so, Jesus had very little faith, for He faced a great deal of trouble in His life, including final execution. His verdict upon it all was, "In the world ye shall have tribulation"—that is the simple, realistic fact: "but be of good cheer, I have overcome the world"—that is the extra fact of faith.

Tribulation *and* triumph—triumph in and through tribulation. This is Christian victory. Jesus gave us no guarantee against trouble, but against defeat. Like all men, Christians face sickness, treachery, hard circumstance, old age, death. But Christians meet these things victoriously.

And this is because there are, in every situation, two factors: there is what happens, and there is how I take what happens. This is why character may always be superior to circumstance. I cannot always control what happens; I can nearly always control how I take what happens. But how I take what happens goes back to what kind of person I am, and what kind of belief I have about life as a whole. If the whole scheme of life is not a scheme at all but a chaos, if there is no thread of purpose running through it all but only confusion, then my misfortunes are just part of the general mess. But if God is, and if life is His creation, with meaning in the middle of it, then I may hope to discover a pattern which will both give coherence to it all and help to interpret any one event in the unfoldment. Then may happen that climax of faith which enabled St. Paul to say, "All things work together for good to them that love God." (R. S. V.: "In everything God works for good with those who love Him.")

Take an ever-present problem like alcoholism. Here is a man (or woman) for whom alcohol is poison. He cannot touch it, yet in his weakness he wants it desperately.

He is born allergic to alcohol. What shall he do with this plaguing, cursing tendency? He can give in to it and become a simple drunkard; or he can face his need with the help of other alcoholics, and get mastery over it. How many have told me they almost thank God they are alcoholics, because if they had not been they would still be trying to run their lives without God—their need threw them back on Him.

Or take a crippling illness. I think of a paralyzed man named Henry. He broke his health trying to care for a huge family of dependent relatives. He is poor; he has to be fed and cared for in every way, being absolutely helpless. But Henry, who was not born a Christian, became a Christian through the friendship of a minister whom I know well. He stuck to him through thick and thin till Henry found his Saviour. For years he has had to lie almost motionless on his bed. But his soul is not motionless. He is reading and praying and pouring out waves of love and concern to people, as many as he knows. His body is tragic; but I wish the souls of the rest of us were in as good condition. He faced a tragic situation, but he met that situation gloriously. I believe that nothing short of faith can help a man do that. And I believe faith can help us to face anything we are meant to face, and to do it with grace and good will and creative imagination. "This is the victory that overcomes the world, even our faith."

The final sorrow, or the final victory, is death. How do you meet death? Do you heap it over with as expensive flowers as you can buy? Do you expose the body of your beloved as if that poor outworn overcoat were really he? Do you fill yourself with drugs or drink, so that you can bear up at the funeral? There is no sin in tears: Jesus cried when His friend Lazarus died. But it seems to me there is great sin in not meeting death in a Christian fashion. I have been hearing of late of several people who have almost passed over the dividing line of death, but have been brought back to life possibly by a lingering consciousness of unfinished work or by the prayers of others. All of them speak about the light they see on the Other Side, about the unutterable beauty of the glimpse they had of it. We do not need human evidences of it. Our Lord's Resurrection is our best proof. We can hardly believe in the love of God as He revealed it, and then believe that at death all of life is dashed to pieces and nothingness. As our faith becomes for us the passionate center of our lives, and we gladly accept the Christian belief about immortality, death becomes a further experience in life. We may not long for it, but we surely do not dread it. We almost take it casually, though we surely must not take the preparation for it casually.

Near Great Barrington, Massachusetts, is a wonderful community called Gould Farm. Will and Agnes Gould began it more than thirty years ago, as a place for nervously and emotionally distressed people, and it has served a noble purpose. Some twenty-five or more years ago, Will contracted pneumonia from fighting a fire in one of their barns, and died. His wife is a very great Christian, and I wrote her not long afterwards and asked how she was feeling about it all. She wrote me something like this: "I have not had anything like a communication from Will, though I constantly feel his love and interest in the farm. If anything has 'come over' to me, it has been something like this: 'Don't make too much of this, my dear—not very much has happened.'" The implication of ongoing, unbroken life in that is, I think, profoundly Christian. When Dr. F. B. Meyer, one of the great preachers of England a couple of generations ago, heard that he had a fatal disease, he wrote to someone that the doctors had given him but three days to live. "Don't trouble to write," he said, "we'll meet in the morning." Can anybody but a Christian meet death in that kind of calm confidence?

The human body is meant to be sacramental. It is to be used for God's ends and purposes. The reason why drink or drugs or often tobacco or any other kind of excess is wrong is not because you can isolate it and say that this in itself is sinful, but because it does not contribute to any great purpose in life and may hinder it. A lot of sin nestles in the flesh, and St. Paul is right when he says, "The flesh warreth against the spirit." But all the instincts of the body, particularly the sex instinct, are God-given and are meant to be God-used. The instrument He chose to continue human life in the world was never meant to be the filthy thing many people have made of it by excess and misuse and promiscuity. Sex can be sacramental, and so can the other uses of the human body.

Christians regard nature sacramentally. Nature put in first place, in God's place, always betrays man, for nature is not first in the original scheme of things. But nature looked upon as God's handiwork, filled with His glory and wonder, continuing to manifest His continuing creation, is a vast sacrament which manifests Him. Gardens, sunsets, oceans, waterfalls, stars, galaxies, and the seemingly limitless universe are part of the "garment of God." Baron von Hugel insisted that nature must be the "soil of grace." Flowers are not earth, but you get no flowers without earth. Grace grows in the ground of nature, and we ought to love the world and the universe for its vast manifestation of Him.

But come closer to home. The things that interest and captivate the average American are business and politics. That's where his heart is. He makes and sells something. Or he holds office somewhere in a village or city or state or the national government. Men often let these things become God's rival for first place in life, because they enjoy them so, and give their best attention to them. Are they natural enemies to God? I believe God means them also to be transformed into His instruments. How, you ask?

There was a boiler-room superintendent in a public utilities plant not far from New York, a huge hulk of a man with a hand like a ham. There were Negroes, Italians, Poles working in the plant. When one of them did what he didn't like, he laid him up against the coal pile. Fear and therefore accidents were rife. One day the superintendent heard a man talk in church about a transforming experience of Christ. He went to talk to him, and that talk changed his life. Back in the plant there was a change of spirit. Fear disappeared. In seven years they did not have an accident. That is making a sacrament of industry, when a man's own changed spirit changes the spirit of the place where he works. Tens of thousands of men in management and labor need to be changed and learn how this is done; for, I say it reverently, business and industry and politics are meant to be the channel of the Spirit of God, just like the bread and wine on God's altars. Only men and women with Christ's spirit can effect that transformation.

Do not give in to the prevailing pagan skepticism about material things. Lift them to God for His blessing and give them to Him for His use—houses, cars, money, offices, business, everything. One day I was walking up Fifth Avenue, New York, with a clergyman friend. He looked up at the high buildings and said, "This is what makes our work impossible." I said, "What?" He said, "All this steel and stone." I said, "I don't agree with you. It ought to make life better for everybody that we can live efficiently. The trouble is that the material creation man has produced is bigger than his own soul. If his soul were bigger than his buildings, we should tread these city streets, and walk through these granite caverns, as if they were cathedral aisles. The trouble is not with things, it is with man's wrong way of regarding them and using them." We ought to look upon all things in the light of the fact that in Christ God took a human body and wore it for thirty-three years. That ought to change everything we think and feel about matter. There is nothing the matter with matter. C. S. Lewis says, "God loves matter. He made it."

Christians have a special way of regarding human life and of dealing with other people.

First, they think differently about themselves. Pagans seek to hold a high regard for themselves through the sheer thrust of ego, and want others to share it for the same reason. Jesus said, "Love thy neighbour *as thyself*." How can we love ourselves in the right way? Caring for the body, yes. Making ourselves as capable as possible, yes. But principally by looking on ourselves as God's agents to do His will. Insofar as I do that, I fulfill my own destiny. I must look on other people as ends. I must look on myself largely as means. This should mean I do not think much about myself at all, except to try to keep in shape and in line to do God's will and work. The whole end of life is to do God's will. Because he knew this and lived accordingly, St. Paul could say (I Cor. 4.3–4), "With me it is a very small thing that I should be judged of you, or of man's judgment: yea, I judge not mine own self . . . but he that judgeth me is the Lord." That is, he really stood, not in man's opinion (for one's friends are likely to be sentimental and one's critics harsh), nor in his own opinion (for we are likely to be either too easy or sometimes too hard on ourselves), but in the opinion of God. And what is God's opinion of us? A father told a child, "I always love you, but I do not always love the things you do." I think that is not far from God's opinion of us, except that He sees our sins with absolute clarity and truth, and loves us with absolute compassion and pity. So don't form your opinion of yourself from men's opinions, though you can learn much from them, not least from your severest critics; and don't form your opinion by your own view of yourself, for you will play up your virtues and achievements, and play down your sins and failures. Let God be the whole Judge. Then you will see yourself as you are, and keep seeking the transformation He wants to effect.

Second, Christians think differently about other people. Pagans are often amusing and delightful people, but the farther removed they are from some sort of Christian influence, the more they regard other people as means for their own ends, instead of as ends in themselves. Dr. Reuel Howe says that people were meant to be loved, and things were meant to be used; and we have gotten that turned right around, so that we love things, and use people. I believe that almost all right human relations have been directly or indirectly influenced by the Christian spirit, and that the only way in which we can produce right human relations is by letting God into every relationship.

Many years ago an old United States Senator was talking to me. He had had a lot of money, and lost it, but his wife went on spending it. What to do? I said, "Senator, you have lived a lot longer than I. But I believe if you could really bring God in on the situation, it would clear up. So many human relations are like dots at the end of a line, and they ought to be like base-angles at the bottom of a triangle, with God at the top. If, instead of trying to work out your problems in the horizontal, you would go up to God, and she would go up to God . . ." He finished the sentence himself, "Then she wouldn't put anything over on me, and I wouldn't put anything over on her!" This happened just after the present form of dollar bill was issued. He drew a dollar from his pocket and said, "The Founding Fathers knew about the triangle. Look at the pyramid of the Great Seal, with the Eye of God at the top!" And there it was, and there it is. You carry it round in your pocket. Let's begin carrying it round in our minds and hearts and relationships!

This is the answer for husband and wife. You know the story about the man and woman who went into church, and went up to the altar, and the minister made them one. Then they went out and got in the car, and the question was, Which one? Whose will shall prevail? Sometimes married life is smooth enough. Again it gets a snarl in it. The real question never is, Who is right? but What is right? In a misunderstanding or disagreement, both sides need to realize the partiality and incompleteness and selfishness of all human viewpoints, and then in common to seek the mind of God. Maybe it concerns how to spend a vacation, or what to do with a windfall of a hundred dollars, or how to handle a difficult child. You can have many a quarrel over such things. But God has always a way. Drop the argument, and go apart and pray for a while. When you meet, pray together; and the chances are, you will come to the right conclusion. The saying is true: the family that prays together stays together.

It is the answer for parents and children. The best way to avoid the frequent clash between them is for the children to know that the parents have Someone to whom they are accountable, also. The parental will does not become the final authority, but God. When parents are wrong, they need to tell their children so. A great deal of psychological confusion in children comes from their sense of outraged justice: they know the parent is as guilty as themselves, yet they have no way of redress. And how shall a parent enforce something which is clearly right? Sometimes it must be by a clear order and the expectation of obedience on the part of the child. But we want to include our children in these decisions, to let them become responsible as soon as may be. A child of seven announced one morning she was not going to church. Her father said, "Just talk it over with God, and let Him tell you. Whatever He says is all right with me." The child prayed alone for a little while, and came back saying, "He didn't tell me I had to go." The father said nothing. The child walked away to play with another child, and did not go to church. Later in the day she said to her father, "I had a bad time today. I don't think I'll stay away from church again." Now the truth is, she was not listening to God, but to her own desires; but she had to find out by trying it that "the way of the transgressor is hard," and I am convinced we need to let children find it out and not decide all questions for them. Prayer, which opens the mind and heart to God, and lets His Voice speak in His own still, small, yet usually quite perceptible way, will bring light such as no human discussion can bring.

What about human relations when they have gone wrong? Is there any way of righting them again? Here there are two things that need to be said.

The first concerns the confession of our own wrong. For two people to find reconciliation after estrangement, the first step is toward justice. There is somewhere a middle ground of right, from which probably both have strayed. We must be willing to see even the little amount of right in the other fellow, and we must be willing to see perhaps the large amount of wrong in ourselves. We tend to keep on emphasizing to ourselves the magnitude of the other person's wrong. Hope dawns when we perceive our own. The only really "impossible" people are the people who are always right, for nobody is always right, including ourselves. We may not be able to get them to budge, but we can budge. We can make the first move. We can confess we are wrong in spirit, even if we hold to the truths we have expressed. That melts what is adamant in us, and gives the Spirit of God and of reconciliation a chance. I go so far as to say that until a man or woman has learned to admit his or her own sins, Christianity has not yet begun. For by the time most of us turn about, and seek God, we are deep in sin—self-will, pride, determination to have our way and keep up our pretense of being right. Innocence is gone forever. Entirely right we shall never be. The only way we can ever begin to be partly right is to admit where we have been partly wrong. None of us is ever converted absolutely to the point of sinlessness; the next thing to it is the honesty which admits how far short of it we are.

There is the story of a boy whose father was always getting after him about something. The boy had a Christian experience and came home and the old man began climbing him, and the boy said, "You know, Dad, maybe you're right." And his father said, "Maybe I'm wrong!" Surely this is what Jesus meant by "turning the other cheek." Expose yourself entirely to the other person. Give him the chance to say to you, "That's just what I've been telling you!" He may say that; but he may say, "I guess I have not been too good myself." Right there the Spirit of God can enter in. Christians, real Christians, have learned how to admit where they are wrong.

The second thing to say concerns forgiveness. Just a dry admission of our own wrong won't bring about reconciliation: there must be in our hearts a desire for it. There is nothing about which Jesus talked more than forgiveness. And every day of our lives we say something that ought to keep us in the right spirit at all times: "Forgive us our trespasses, as we forgive those who trespass against us." We ask God to deal with our sins as we deal with the sins of others. It would go hard with some of us if He did. For we are relentless and obdurate: we will not forgive. In the end, of course, this does more harm to us than to those against whom we hold a grievance. It makes people sick to be unforgiving. Unforgiveness lying in the mind is worse than poison lying in the body. You say, What should I do? The first thing is not something to "do," but something to recognize and feel. You can't "do" anything effective till your feeling is more right. Let us say the other person is just as obdurate as you, and has no idea of asking for forgiveness: what can you do? You can pray and surrender the resentment in your own heart. You can feel a sense of "forgivingness" before you can extend to him an actual "forgiveness." You can see the sin and shame of your own relentlessness and give it up. That is first.

Then what? Now perhaps the wrong he has done you is real. He has taken something that was yours, looked at your private letters, lied about you to others, taken a business advantage over you, pulled a fast one. It is right for you to make your point. I do not think we ought to let people just get away with things like that, for if so they will do it again: we want them to learn something out of this, as well as ourselves. So we shall make our point with them. It must be said with as little rancor as possible, but the truth needs to be said. It must be said in love, for then you will leave the way open for the other person to say what he believes the truth to be. You will work your way together if there is real forgiveness in your own heart.

There are two final things to be said about the way Christians live.

The first concerns our Christian service to the world. The whole Christian enterprise has been one long service to mankind. Our education, our hospitals, even our theaters, were originally the Church's affair. I believe a good historic case could be made for stating that the impulse back of practically every move for the betterment of man in the past twenty centuries has been a Christian motive, directly or indirectly. This nation is an island of freedom and plenty in a world of tyranny and poverty. Unless we enable that poor world to achieve better means of livelihood, of education, of agriculture, of health, Communism will scoop it into its net by promises which will never be fulfilled but the mere stating of which will be enough to bring it within the Communist orbit—and Communism can never be stopped while it goes on winning further conquests of nations by its ideology. There are therefore two motives in our world service today. There is the simple, Christian motive of helping those who cannot help themselves—and if we had followed that motive years ago, and all America had been as interested in foreign missions as it was in foreign trade, the face of the world might look quite different today. And then there is the motive of plain expediency, that if we do not help these people, they will be lost to liberty and won to slavery. It was Lenin who said that when Communism has control of all the underprivileged races, the revolution will really begin. For once, goodness and self-interest coincide in a most obvious fashion. If you are not thinking about China and India and Africa and the Near East, as much as you are thinking about your business and your town and your home and family, you are blind and stupid. I would even say you were helping the enemies of America. For they are thinking of these places. If we get there with our know-how in time, we can keep these nations free and in the democratic orbit; but if we fail, they will go Communist as sure as death. Dr. Frank

Laubach says we have about four years in which to work, for they are going Communist at the rate of 100,000,000 a year. What is your share and project in world service?

The second thing to say concerns the Christian's resource. We cannot do any of these things in our own strength. It is Christ that does the work in us and through us. The people who really believe that are always enthusiastic people. Faith and enthusiasm are scarcely distinguishable. And enthusiastic people are always cheerful and happy people. Are you? The churches are full of people who have not found the full joy of the Christian life, and who therefore are not one fraction of the people they might be if they had let Him spark their whole personalities with His joy and creative power. They keep saying their prayers and going to church in a perfunctory sort of way. Much of it acts almost like a vaccination against getting any real religion. They are like a man going into a shower bath with a raincoat and a bathing cap and rubber boots on. You don't know whether they are there to get religion or to steel themselves further against it. Hence William James said religion is either a dull habit or an acute fever.

What we need is more people for whom it is an acute fever—a pervasive, lifelong, creative, useful enthusiasm that never tires of asking to be put into the full stream of God's will. People like that know the victory we have been speaking about, over trouble and circumstance. They find and make nature and the material sacramental. They work out their human relations with God as Third Party to them all. And they pour out of what God has given them. "Freely ye have received: freely give." The world needs people like that as it never did before. And one of the greatest things any of us can do for the poor and sick world in which we live is to become a committed, enthusiastic, sharing Christian.

8

CHRISTIAN WITNESS

Most people owe their Christian faith, especially when it becomes sharp and effective, to other persons. Not long ago I was listening to a man in an Alcoholics Anonymous meeting give his own story. He had been a proud materialist, and it took a long time for him to get the "spiritual" angle of A. A. or to admit that God had anything to do with recovery. He took the "program" and went along well for some months. Then he was asked to lead a meeting, and did it. Afterwards a dumpy little English seaman who was in the meeting came up to him and said, "You didn't say a thing about God in the meeting." He made some excuse. The Britisher took him by the lapels and said, "You are evading Him!" He got so much under conviction from this that he went on another spree, which showed how shallow was his first commitment. But when he came out of it, his pride was broken. He had to admit that he needed God, that God and God alone had the answer for him. The word of that fat little Englishman had done it. Thank God for people with that kind of simple, friendly courage!

A friend of mine recalls hearing Dr. Winnington-Ingram, one of the greatest of the Bishops of London, say that God evidently intended that salvation should be made known to man through man; that there is no evidence that God has changed His mind about this plan; and that until we accept this responsibility, nothing can happen in the world with regard to the coming of the Kingdom of God.

Think back—has not every spiritual idea or belief or advance in your life come through some person? It came through your mother or father. It came through a Sunday-school teacher. It came through a Christian day-school teacher, or a missionary at home on furlough, or a sermon you heard, one idea of which took root and grew in your mind. I shall never forget the first time I ever heard a preacher voice the thought that "Thy will be done" did not mean *resignation*, but *co-operation*. That opened up a new world of thought to me, and led eventually to my own decision to try to surrender my life to God and His will.

Real religion is a stream of power which has its rise in God, flows from Him to others and through them to us, or to us and through us to others. It is not just an attitude or a belief in a set of theological or ethical propositions: it is a stream of power, like electricity. God is like a great, hidden dynamo. Christ and His Church are like outlets where we can tap His power. Surrender, conversion, promising to "follow Him" are like plugging in your personal wire to the outlet. And prayer is like turning on the power which comes from the divine dynamo. That is too mechanical to be exact, for God and we are persons, not machines; but I want you to feel that the power of God through faith is just as definite, just as tangible, yes, just as usable (if you use it the right way) as electricity. The trouble with many people is that they are dead-ends of power, when they ought to be transmitters of it. They are glad for what religion has done for them, but they give up on getting it across to others. It comes to them, but there it stops, when they ought to be factors in a circuit which is not completed till other people come in touch with the same power of God as we know God in Christ.

But the everlasting question is, How?

We know people who try to do this work, and do it in most unfortunate ways. They come at you quoting Scripture, or asking if you're saved, or whether you've had the Second Blessing. One fellow, asked whether he'd had the Second Blessing, said, No—he'd been bothered by these Second Blessing people to such an extent that he'd asked God for the First Blessing and the Third Blessing, but he'd be grateful if the Lord would just skip that Second Blessing, as it made people such a nuisance! We don't want to be like that. Our language must be the language of ordinary men about ordinary affairs, remembering that when God uttered the Word of Christ, that Word was in terms of our common human life. We must begin, as Jesus began with the Woman at the Well, not with our answer but with their situation: He talked first about the water she had come to draw, and then went on to compare what He wanted to give to her to this same water. It was a normal progression from the natural to the supernatural. He did not begin with religion, and get to life: He began with life, and went to religion, and then got back to life again. It was always the way He worked. So must we. People are not won by our hurling doctrines at their heads—they are won by sympathy and understanding, by naturalness and friendliness, by watching the way we take life and meet it, above all by our courtesy and manners and friendliness as we meet them. Natural language and a natural approach come first.

Some say that our only way to witness is through example. That is a good and essential way of witness. What we are speaks so loud men can't hear what we say, as Emerson said. Courage in the midst of trouble and suffering, faith when the going is hard, integrity about keeping promises and paying bills, the obvious manifestation of power beyond our own—all this is essential. Three clergymen that I know have lost greatly loved children in the prime of their lives. Each of them met his crisis with superb serenity and faith, with a victory that bespoke the Presence and power of God as nothing else could. That did more for their people's belief in immortality than a dozen sermons on it.

But there is a limit to this. A good life can testify to belief in some kind of Higher Power. But for Christians the distinctive thing is not that there is a God, and therefore we ought to live like brothers: it is that God came into the world in Christ, and redeemed the world by His death, and that He rose again from the dead and is alive forevermore. Christians come to God through Christ. We believe that in Him God did those "mighty acts" which prove what kind of God He is. I do not know any mere example that can quite tell men that we believe God spoke in Christ to all men forever, or that Christ is God Incarnate, or that the Cross saves men from their sins, or that the Resurrection is the crowning article of faith for Christians. It would be insolently conceited for me to think that the influence of my life alone could ever give witness of these great things to other people, yet they are the verities in which the Christian faith stands. As I cannot render on my piano anything but the echo and reminder of the symphony which the Philharmonic can really play, so my single example can be but the faintest echo of the profound harmonies of the Gospel. I cannot play what the Philharmonic can play, but I can tell people about the Philharmonic and get them to listen for themselves. What I cannot reproduce adequately, I can nevertheless talk about and point to. It is so with Christ. My faith can go much farther than my life. I am ashamed at how little of my faith I put to work in my life, but I am not in the least ashamed of my Lord and my faith in Him. My example might encourage people to do better. Or it might cause them to think that this was all there is. I must point them to Him, not me.

There is another thing. An example may inspire us, or it may make us say, "Well, he is like that, he always has been." We say of a believing person that he or she is not troubled by temper or nerves, as we are, but is just by nature a happier, more trusting person. We may admire someone's serenity or courage or hopefulness, but it may not occur to us that he had to fight for what he has, work at it, grow in it. Two men influenced my life profoundly. One was perhaps the finest character I ever knew: I admired him extravagantly, and drew great inspiration from him, but I felt he was so far above me it was hopeless to try to do much about it. The other was a less noble character, but the explanation and articulation of his faith was much more clear, and for this reason he did more to change the direction of my life.

Dr. John Oliver Nelson says that believing Christians

fall into one of five categories: (1) the strong silent type, who say they just "live their faith"; (2) those who make casual remarks, such as saying they have been to church, or say their prayers; (3) the "won't-you-attend" type, who invite people to come to services, meetings, etc., where others say what they do not have the courage to say themselves; (4) those who talk publicly, speaking at meetings and leading them, talking with a crowd as they do not quite have the courage to do across a table with an individual; and (5) those who share their personal faith, in informal conversational ways, being sensitive to the other person's needs, giving to others the real core of their own faith. Which category do you fall into?

Dr. Elton Trueblood says that we need three things: philosophy, program, and passion; without these three the life we prize will be overwhelmed, with or without a war. Now our philosophy is the whole Christian view of God and man and the universe, and without that basic belief we shall flounder in a sea of merely personal reflections. Our program is that of a Church alive and on the march to win every life and capture every area of human existence for Christ. Our passion is the enthusiasm we feel for Christ, the drive and energy He communicates to us, and which we communicate to others, enthusiasm being one of the most contagious things in the world. The thing must have happened to us, or be in process of happening to us—otherwise we are like a blind man describing a sunset, or one that is tone-deaf telling about a symphony. We must know at least the rudiments of the faith. We must have the beginnings of a plan for life and for the world—we can all share in that which the whole Church shares. And we must have a passion to get it over.

Let me suggest five concrete steps:

1. Get a point of contact. The only way to do that is to like people, and to live on their territory and take an interest in their interests. Don't try smart sales tricks: pray for simple, genuine love for them, find out what they are interested in, and get them to tell you about it. Something human may need to happen between you two as individuals, before anything can be done spiritually. A woman brought her husband to lunch with my wife and me one day, with the idea that we convert him. He was about as eager as a puppy drawing back on a leash with his paws scraping every inch of the sidewalk. We soon found that he was interested in two subjects: deep-sea fishing and Woodrow Wilson. My wife is a good fisherman, and asked the questions that drew him out on that, and he kept things going for about two courses. My enthusiasm for the great democratic President is as great as his, so I drew him out on that, and by that time he had talked his way through the meal, and it was almost time

for him to leave for the theater at two o'clock. But in the time left, it was very easy to pick up from the kind of faith Woodrow Wilson had in democracy, and where it came from, and go on to talk about the relation between freedom and faith. In a few moments he was greatly interested, and was helping us formulate plans for getting this across to more people. If we had started in at the beginning on his conversion, we should have lost him entirely. Contact with people of this sort is much more a matter of *living* than it is of *selling*. They will judge our "stuff" by what kind of people we are. So get a point of contact with their life and interests.

2. Move in from the general to the personal as soon as it is natural. Everybody is exercised about the world, and fears for the future of freedom, and thinks a general revival would be a good thing. This is only wishful thinking until each of us makes some move of his own. "We certainly do need *something*" is the first groping step toward a dynamic faith. We might then say, "This means you and I need something, doesn't it?" And then, lest he become too self-conscious by our turning it personally, we might say, "You know, you could do a lot about this if you got going." To which the frequent reply is, "It would have to happen to me first," or "I couldn't do it as I am." Then we may say, "That is probably true. That was what I found. . . ." And there is a natural opening

147

to give our own personal witness of how we found God. Not too long, no "total recall," just in a way to intrigue and interest him. Down in these deep places of the human spirit, we all think and feel much alike. In T. S. Eliot's *The Cocktail Party* the psychiatrist Hartcourt-Reilly says to Edward, "All cases are unique, and very similar to others." And it is the philosopher Dr. W. E. Hocking who says that religion becomes universal at the point where it becomes most peculiarly personal. Remember that everybody likes to talk about himself, no matter how much he swears he doesn't. Give him the chance. Ask only such questions as will open him up—personal, but not too personal, not "nosy." Keep ready to speak out of your own heart and life. That is the way in which people come really to know one another. Be a good listener, and don't talk too much.

A young businessman came to talk about the youth work in his church which he led. He wanted help on how to make it more vital. He had a folder in his hand. He said the group was not as vital as it might be. We never touched the folder, we were too busy touching him. I told him about some groups I had tried to lead when I was at his place, and how they fizzled out. Then I told him about other kinds of vital groups, and said that the difference lay, not primarily in a different method or technique, but in a change in me. I found this fellow had some beliefs and convictions, but no power—just like masses of church people everywhere. He couldn't get his faith across to others because he did not have enough of it. We got down into the deep places of his life, he found he could talk freely and confidentially about everything that went on (and some of it didn't match very well with leading a young people's group), and we wound up on our knees as for the first time he surrendered everything he could to Christ. The difference in him today is striking. His program for young people includes a factor it never included before: personal commitment to Jesus Christ. We need to move from the general admission of need, or the responsibility already assumed, to the personal life of the person. He told me that no minister had ever taken time to talk with him this way. There is something the matter with that picture.

3. Help him to make a moral inventory, to analyze himself spiritually. Most of us will admit that we are "miserable offenders," but that does no good unless we are specific about it. We must get all this, not in a vacuum, but in relation to a deep commitment to Christ—how does He see this or that? And also in relation to our going to work for Him—what constitutes "sin" for a person who knows he ought to be winning other people to Christ? Drinking, throwing away selfish money, shyness and self-consciousness, failure to think through what

we really believe, the ineffectiveness of not knowing what to say or do in the face of an open spiritual opportunity—such things as these become as sinful as adultery or hatred or theft. The "I never hurt anybody" kind of Christian has got to give place to the kind of Christian that knows how to get his faith across to other people and help them. Don't let them draw a little circle around their petting parties, or their business crookednesses, or their basic materialism, and look at these things by themselves: get them to look at these things in the light of a full commitment to Christ and the desire to be used by Him in making faith live for others. Sin is anything that keeps me from God, or from being effective for God.

Another young college man came for a personal talk. While making application at a graduate school, he had sat outside the dean's office with a student from another university. It was not long till they were talking, not about the relative merits of their two universities, but about the very vital work which had been started on the campus where the second of these men studied. It intrigued and thrilled the first one. He soon after came to learn more about this movement of the spirit that was permeating the colleges. I found out he had a strong church background and was heading for the ministry eventually. But as we talked, his problems came out: defeat in the area of affections and sex; nervous tension over which he seemed to have no control; aggressiveness which often turned to hostility. He looked all right on the outside: but within were great insecurity and need. We faced these things together, and he surrendered them to God. Within a few days he was talking with other people on his campus, and had a group going there. This all came from the fact that someone helped him to face himself and get squared away on what God wanted of him.

4. Help him to make a Christian decision. Of course the world is full of people who have made no Christian decision, but the Church is also full of them. They got in somehow, baptized as babies, confirmed in early adolescence, and continuing on in a lackluster, dull kind of way as church members. *This is what is the matter with the Church.* You can't cure it by drives or study groups or sales campaigns; you can cure it only by conversions, deep and on a huge scale, beginning with bishops and clergy, with vestrymen and the laymen and women who help us do the organized work of the Church, but many of whom would be helpless in the presence of a person in obvious spiritual need or who asked for spiritual help. Confirmation ought to be the outside of which conversion is the inside. Sometimes it is. Often it is not. Many of us in the Church have got to go back to the place where we dropped the stitch and

pick it up. We need to work with each other and help each other into this deeper commitment. And there are thousands of pagans who do not "get it" when we tell them some one element in the faith, or give them a bit of the truth, but they *do* get it when we tell them God asks them to make as complete a commitment as possible.

Self-surrender is the handle by which we can take hold of real conversion. We are not out, first of all, to interest people in the Church, or in its work. We are not out to make more lackluster Christians like the many we have. We are out to help people find Christ in all His regal claims, and in all the adventure and joy and reality that attend a real commitment to Him. Many think of conversion as something very exceptional, which only comes to a few people. That is the way churchpeople fool themselves, evade the challenge, and miss the joy and power of real Christian conversion. When I realized how powerless I was to do this very thing I am urging on you—get my faith over to someone else—I realized how badly something was needed, in my own life. I had done most of the things the Church expects a young man to do; I had not done the one thing the Gospel expects everybody to do. Jesus said, "Ye *must* be born again." I thank God for a man who did not take me for granted, but who put that challenge before me when I was teaching in a mission school in China, after I was a postulant for Holy Orders in the Church, ten years after my Confirmation. The best friend you will ever have is the one who helps you to make that decision. It is not enough to ask people to come to church, or to have a little religious discussion with them. There is no sale, there is no transaction, nothing really has happened, till they have made an actual commitment of themselves to Jesus Christ. I dare to say that, if the Church would really learn that, and get people converted before it gets them running through its often admirable routines, we could sweep the world. But our history won't do it, our decency won't do it, our "incomparable liturgy" won't do it. Nothing but the conversion of our hearts, and learning how to pass on to others the reality of Christian faith and life and witness.

5. Give people the next steps to go on with, and grow. They need to be introduced to the Bible and shown how to read it steadily and effectively. They need elementary help in prayer, and daily private devotions, and the assistance of the right kind of books. A good time of devotion and quiet with God every day adds a new dimension to life and gets us in the habit of trying to be in touch with Him all through the day. They need to be helped in coming into vital membership in the Church, whichever one they belong to, taking responsibility, giving regularly, coming regularly, bringing other people and helping

the parson win and train them. In my own Communion, the clergy today are caring for almost exactly twice as many people as they were in 1900, yet the kinds of demands put upon us by the community today are vastly greater. Therefore the necessity of lay people who are good with other people and can help us by calling and by personal work is urgent and ever present. Of course some clergy will never do this kind of work because they do not want to be stormed out of their little ecclesiastical citadels and thrust into the lives of people. Parsons must take the time to win some people all the way through to a vital and radiant and contagious experience, and then to train themselves and their people in this kind of man-to-man work, for which there is no substitute. I would not go far or make much effort just to increase the number of pew-warmers and barnacles that hang on to the shell of the Church. Neither Satan nor Joe Stalin has the slightest fear of them. I do not see how God Himself can possibly use them, for He has only a small fraction of their hearts: the rest belongs to themselves. The Church ought to be such a place that new people brought into it are kept warm and alive and helped to grow till every one of them is a multiplying, reproducing, contagious Christian. Someone said that to g-r-o-w was to "go right on working," not go right on sitting.

Some of this work will be done with individuals, in the way I have been indicating: some of it will be done *through* your job. Remember, business must be redeemed by the injection into it of the Spirit of Christ. It must become sacramental. When we do the daily job differently, that happens. A man came for a few meetings to a small group discussing the way of applying Christianity in daily life. He was a quiet person, and listened. But one day he came up with the fact that he had tried these principles out. He had prayed before an important conference (where tension was likely to arise); it had gone smoothly partly because he was in the right spirit himself; a big sale had gone through. He hastened to say he was not interested in the $20,000 sale so much as in finding that one could be a Christian in the way one conducted oneself and one's business. The spirit of a man like that will spread till it affects others about him. Maybe he'll get a group going in his company. He has taken the first important step of making the company where he works Christian, by becoming a real and not just a nominal Christian himself, and then by letting God work in the office.

Sometimes it comes through the home. You often see the "mustard seed" these days, on women's bracelets and men's watchchains. Do you know the story back of that? A man and wife had had difficulty, and were led to a man of God who helped them find harmony in their home again. It touched them so that they sought some manifestation of faith that would cause comment. Looking through the New Testament, they found faith was compared to a "mustard seed," so the man asked his wife what one looked like. She told him there was one in the pickle jar, and drew it out. He took it to a jeweler to see if it could be caught in a glass drop. He did it, and then began the phenomenal sale of these "mustard seeds." Every one of them ought to be a reminder and an inspiration to a sound and solid home, where Christ is Master.

But in the long run, we find ourselves faced with individuals. They need faith. They need Christ. They need, not just a little more religion, but a real experience of God. That is the kind of faith Dr. Kirsopp Lake was talking about when he said, "Faith is not belief in spite of evidence; it is life in scorn of consequence." We know from all the evidence we have seen and experienced that Jesus Christ is adequate for every human situation, that He who made life can alone redeem and lift it. What He needs in the world is hands and feet, eyes and tongues, that go His errands and do His work. His religion has gone through the world like a benevolent contagion, life impinging on life. That is how it has spread.

A friend of mine has figured out that if every single Christian were a witnessing Christian who won one man a year, in twenty-one years there would be 1,208,576 people won. Continue that figuring, and it would not take long till the world was won. The miss in the calculation is in the Christians you can depend upon. Many will do a bit of church work; few will think through the meaning of a Christian philosophy for life and politics and business today, or learn how to touch individuals for Christ.

The question is: When are you going to get going?

There are two kinds of atoms, as I understand it, the U-235 atom, which, when struck by a neutron, "fisses," and the U-238 atom, which absorbs the neutron without "fissing." In nature there are 142 U-238 atoms to one U-235 atom. And the atomic physicist had to change that proportion. Now the world and the Church are full of spiritual U-238's. They won't go off, no matter what hits into them. It will take, not an atomic physicist, but God Almighty Maker of Heaven and Earth to bring to bear upon them the impact that will make them explode. If we will bring these U-238 lives and souls of ours to Him, and ask Him to do it, He will do it.

We need to see in this world a release of spiritual power comparable to the power of atomic fission. It must be spiritual power, and it must be constructive power. Every man, woman, and child that calls himself a Christian in these days must offer himself to God to be used in this vast, urgent spiritual warfare. In the end, only Christianity has been on the side of man. It must be eventually the winning side, if we have learned by now "the things which belong to our peace."

6-27-54 CFW.

Set in Linotype Janson
Format by Robert Cheney
Manufactured by The Haddon Craftsmen, Inc.
Published by HARPER & BROTHERS, New York